The Church
Anticipating the Kingdom's Appearing
Studies in 1 & 2 Timothy

Written by
James T. Draper, Jr.
and
Gene Mims

Adult January Bible Study
LifeWay Press
Nashville, TN

How to Become a Christian

HIGHWAY TO HEAVEN

You won't find it on a map, but a highway to heaven does exist. "The Roman Road" is explained in the Book of Romans in the Bible, and it tells how to go to heaven.

The road begins at Romans 1:16: "For I am not ashamed of the gospel, because it is God's power for salvation to everyone who believes." God is the source for our journey to heaven. He gives power for salvation to all who believe.

We need God's power because we have a problem with sin. "For all have sinned and fall short of the glory of God" (Romans 3:23). "Sin" means missing the mark or missing God's intended destination for us. None of us can reach that destination on his or her own because everyone is a sinner.

When we work, we earn money. Sin earns wages as well—wages of death. Because God loves all sinners, He has provided another route: "For the wages of sin is death, but the gift of God is eternal life in Christ Jesus our Lord" (Romans 6:23).

The highway to heaven is found in Romans 10:9: "If you confess with your mouth, 'Jesus is Lord,' and believe in your heart that God raised Him from the dead, you will be saved." We need to confess our sin and ask God for forgiveness. To confess Jesus as Lord involves agreeing with God about your sin and your need for salvation. You must repent of your sin, turning away from the direction in life in which you are going. To "believe in your heart" is to place your faith in Jesus, trusting that He died on the cross to pay for your sins. "But God proves His own love for us in that while we were still sinners Christ died for us" (Romans 5:8).

If you would like to have salvation in Jesus Christ, sincerely pray a prayer like this one: "Dear God, I confess to You my sin and need for salvation. I turn away from my sin and place my faith in Jesus as my Savior and Lord. Amen."

Share your faith in Jesus with a Christian friend or pastor. Becoming a Christian is your first step on the lifelong road of spiritual growth and service God desires for you. Follow Christ in believer's baptism by immersion and join a local church.

© Copyright 2003 LifeWay Press
All rights reserved.

No part of this work may be reproduced or transmitted in any form or by any means, electronic or mechanical, including photocopying and recording, or by any information storage or retrieval system, except as may be expressly permitted in writing by the publisher. Requests for permission should be addressed in writing to LifeWay Press, One LifeWay Plaza, Nashville, TN 37234-0175.

ISBN: 0-6330-7990-1

This book is a resource in the Leadership and Skill Development category of the Christian Growth Study Plan.

Dewey Decimal Classification Number: 268.1
Subject Heading: Bible, N.T.

Printed in the United States of America

Leadership and Adult Publishing
LifeWay Church Resources
One LifeWay Plaza
Nashville, TN 37234-0175

We believe the Bible has God for its author; salvation for its end; and truth, without any mixture of error, for its matter and that all Scripture is totally true and trustworthy. The 2000 statement of *The Baptist Faith and Message* is our doctrinal guideline.

Unless other wise indicated, all Scripture quotations are from the *Holman Christian Standard Bible®*, © Copyright 2000 by Holman Bible Publishers. Used by permission.

The Church
Anticipating the Kingdom's Appearing
Studies in 1 & 2 Timothy

Session 1
Making Disciples and Maturing Believers (1 Tim. 1:1—3:13)

Session 2
Maintaining Truth and Multiplying Ministries (1 Tim. 4:1—6:21)

Session 3
Ministering in the World (2 Tim. 1:1—2:26)

Session 4
Ministering in the Last Days (2 Tim. 3:1—4:22)

from the editor

What is the "right" worship style and the role and function of men and women in the church? Are the character and lifestyle of church leaders important? Is sound doctrine vital? What responsibilities do believers have toward other believers? In a world driven to possess wealth, how and why should I seek contentment? How can my church minister effectively? What should be the church's standard for faith and practice? What responsibility does a kingdom-anticipating church have to the world?

Readers will discover answers to these questions and more as they study the Books of 1 and 2 Timothy. These two epistles are earnest pastoral letters from the apostle Paul, a veteran missionary, to a younger colleague Timothy, who was a companion of Paul in his travels. When Paul wrote these letters, he was in Philippi and later in prison. Living at Ephesus at the time, Timothy served as Paul's representative to believers in that city. Written to a young believer in the first century, the message of these two books is as contemporary today as it was then. And that message will help churches become kingdom-anticipating churches filled with Christians who are committed to making disciples, maturing believers, and multiplying their ministries.

This Learner Guide for 2004 January Bible Study is written in an informal, easy-to-read style that helps the reader understand the biblical text without extensive comments. It also has a series of helps to enhance each adult's study. These helps include:

- Text boxes entitled "In Depth" that elaborate on or provide summary information on related chapter topics.
- Two Learning Activities in each chapter. Each activity is integral to the teaching plans in the Leader Guide.
- Sets of questions in each chapter entitled "For Your Consideration." Some questions relate to Bible content. Reflective questions are based on the Scripture passage and call for in-depth thought. Some questions are application questions that help learners focus on the passage's present-day meaning for their lives. These questions can be used in individual or group study and with the Learning Activities can help a group leader stimulate discussion.

Leaders will find further commentary (Expository Notes) and a guide for teaching (Teaching Plans) in the Leader Guide entitled *The Church: Anticipating the Kingdom's Appearing, Studies in 1 and 2 Timothy* (ISBN: 0-6330-79928).

James T. Draper Jr., President of LifeWay Christian Resources, and Gene Mims, President of LifeWay Church Resources, wrote the Learner Guide.

The church's message: A Transforming gospel

Scripture	1 Timothy 1:1-20

They're three of the scariest words you'll ever hear: *"You're in charge."*

You've experienced the feeling, haven't you? It can be at work your first day on the job or first day with new responsibilities, on the ball field your first game as captain, or repeating your marriage vows.

Whatever the outside circumstances, the inside ones are likely to be very much the same: you're basically somewhere between apprehensive and scared to death. Maybe it's your first time in a position of authority. You've studied the theory backwards and forwards but you don't have any practical experience. You seriously doubt your ability to call the shots because you've never done it before. You aren't sure about what action to take in an emergency. And what's more, now everybody brings their problems to *you*.

The realization that it's all in your court is a frightening one. And I think it's safe to say Paul's young friend Timothy was apprehensive about his leadership role when Paul wrote to him in Ephesus from Macedonia.

Providentially for Timothy, he had one of the best teachers anywhere. As an apostle, Paul had actually seen Jesus after the resurrection and was singled out by Him to serve His kingdom. Both Timothy and the

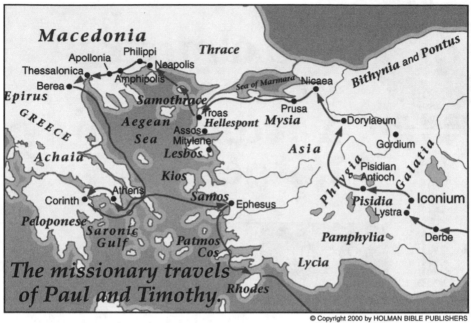

The missionary travels of Paul and Timothy.

Ephesians who read his letter would have been familiar with Paul's Damascus Road conversion, one of the most dramatic and memorable stories in the New Testament (Acts 9). Paul reminded Timothy and the others that he had his office "according to the *command* of God our Savior and of Christ Jesus, our hope" (1 Tim. 1:1).

Not only was Paul fully and forcefully building up Timothy and giving him confidence, but he was raising Timothy's position in the eyes of the Ephesians. Such is the skill of his writing that this transfer is clear to both audiences, describing Timothy as his "true child in the faith" (v. 2).

Christ came into the world to save sinners. This miraculous news is the most important thing you can tell anyone. Remember the first time you ever tried to share the gospel with someone? I remember mine. I felt hopelessly inadequate. But telling someone about Jesus is a lot like tying your shoe. Remember teaching your children or nephews or siblings? "Watch me. Here's how you do it. Hold this loop here and wrap the other string around like this." That's just the way it works with learning how to share the gospel: watch and learn from a patient and seasoned mentor. Or, as in Timothy's case, read a letter from a mentor. Paul was reminding Timothy, "Here's what I did. And here's what happened to me as a result."

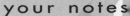

The second step to tying your shoe—or teaching the gospel—is, "OK, you've seen me do it. Now you have a go at it and I'll help you." *And I'll help you.* Those few words take the fear away. "I'll help you, and if anything goes wrong, I'll be right here to fix it." Let's look at what happens. At the very beginning there was frustration and fear of failure; but then you got to watch the expert and your confidence level went up. Then the expert says, "You try it now." And the fear rises up again because while you've become comfortable at watching, you still don't have any confidence doing it yourself. But the mentor says, "Don't worry,

your notes

Learning Activity

Transformation Identification

Using the chart below, list things in the first column that change or transform. In the second column, list what each thing changes or transforms into. One example is given to help get you started. Be creative.

Caterpillar	Butterfly

I'll be right here. *I won't let you fail.*" And your confidence level goes up again because he's there helping you.

Then the third step is, "Now you do it and I'll watch. You've got it, but I'll be here for encouragement just in case anything unexpected pops up." Deep down you know how to do it, but the fear of failure rises up again at the newness of it all. You feel as if you need some backup, and you get it.

Then the time comes when you're able to do the job confidently on your own. You've got some experience that allows the confidence in you to blossom. And finally, you're the experienced one, ready to make the transition from student and apprentice to teacher and mentor of another circle of Christians.

For Your Consideration
1. What can someone in authority do to best encourage and equip others?

2. What do you think are the most important steps in teaching Christians to share their testimony?

True Doctrine—A Firm Foundation
(1 Tim. 1:1-11)

The main reason Paul left Timothy in Ephesus was to "command certain people not to teach other doctrine or to pay attention to myths and endless genealogies" (1:3-4). Today, just as sharply as in first-century Ephesus, the truth divides people. The deeper the truth, the deeper the division.

Paul reminded Timothy that the goal of his work was "love from a pure heart, a good conscience, and a sincere faith" (v. 5). These are the essential goals of the transforming nature of the gospel of Jesus Christ. They represent the process of transforming sinners—Paul, Timothy, you, me—into saints of the faith. The church and the people dedicated to transforming the lives of nonbelievers will be the ones who do a great work for the kingdom of God.

This means meeting the lost at their point of need, without compromising Christian standards. As Paul went down the list of sinful

Timothy represented a new wave of Christian teachers, carrying the message of the faith to the next generation.

behaviors in 1:9-11, he made it clear that the people who commit these sins were the people Timothy's teaching was for. And although Paul invited these people to accept Christ, he never accepted or approved of their behavior.

Yes, Jesus ate with the prostitutes and tax collectors, but only to lead them away from those practices and to the truth, *not* to affirm or condone their lifestyles. People who argue in favor of homosexuality, marital infidelity, and other sins, saying the Bible makes allowances for these practices, need to read and memorize verses 9-11. As dramatically as the world has changed in 20 centuries, human nature hasn't changed at all.

Paul had to make his message unfailingly clear to his young associate. He and Timothy likely both realized that the simpler the gospel message was, the harder it would be to distort. It's always to somebody's advantage to distort the truth. As Paul reminded him at the end of verse 11, not only does the truth matter, but there's nothing more important.

Have you ever known anybody who thought he knew it all? Timothy and the Ephesians were surrounded by self-proclaimed experts who preached falsehoods about Christ and His message. In a sea of relativism, Timothy was charged with being an island of truth. It was a heavy responsibility.

Learning Activity

My Transformation

Paul proclaimed God's transforming grace. Paul offered the change that had been made in his life as an example of God's transforming power. In the following areas, indicate the level of change that God has made in your life:

	1	10
My wants and desires		
My speech		
My temper/anger		
My lust		
My use of time		
My integrity		
My love		
My patience		
My worship		
My testimony		

Other area of transformation:_____

For Your Consideration (1:1-11)

1. What do you think are the characteristics of a "true child in the faith"? How are these characteristics different today than in Timothy's day?

2. Of all the duties Paul could have assigned Timothy, why do you think he emphasized more than anything else the need to stop false teaching?

3. What was Paul's principal goal in ministry?

4. For what kind of person is God's law meant?

5. On what authority should the law be based?

IN DEPTH

Spiritual Transformation

Jesus Christ came into the world to save sinners. This is the core message of all Christian evangelism, and knowing it in your heart is a spiritually transforming moment unlike any other. The gospel transforms sinners into saints. Paul used himself as an example of this great spiritual change. He and Timothy had dedicated their ministry to repeating that experience in the lives of unsaved Ephesians. Their success—and the success of any ministry outreach—can be measured ultimately by the number of lives it transforms.

6. Paul wrote to Timothy knowing others would be reading his letter. How do you think his letter would have been different if he had known only Timothy would see it?

7. How can you overcome the fear of failure when a big responsibility is shifted from someone else's shoulders to yours?

Paul's Testimony of Faith (1 Tim. 1:12-20)

God's transforming power shines through Paul's testimony. The idea Paul expressed was that "if God can redeem me, He can redeem anybody." Paul reaffirmed the truth that Christ came into the world to save sinners, and insisted he was the worst of the lot (vv. 12-17). To paraphrase his remarks we might say, *Timothy, let this be a lesson to you. Let my example give you faith and confidence. You've seen what happens to people who ignore the gospel message—I have delivered them to Satan to teach them not to blaspheme* (vv. 18-20).

Timothy clearly knew what he ought to be doing, but needed some encouragement to do it. How much we know about Timothy from the way Paul wrote is remarkable. Since Timothy was not generally a take-charge guy, he had a healthy apprehension of being in charge. He was not a natural leader. On top of that he was basically timid. Paul figuratively scooted him forward toward the center of the action. *Don't stand out here on the edge of things,* the wise and experienced apostle seemed to say. *Get in there and defend the truth. Get in there and oppose false teaching with the true message of Christ.*

If you're willing to obey God in whatever He asks you to do, He will see to it that you have all the strength and ability you need to succeed, even in the presence of infamous troublemakers like Hymenaeus and Alexander (v. 20).

In Exodus, when God appeared to Moses and told him he had been chosen to lead the people of Israel to the promised land, Moses felt sure he was not up to the task. But the Lord said to him, "Who made the human mouth? Who makes him mute or deaf, seeing or blind? Is it not I, the Lord? Now go! I will help you speak and I will teach you what to say" (Ex. 4:10-12). The same help was there for Timothy.

Paul spent this first chapter of 1 Timothy setting up the challenges and problems he knew his beloved friend was dealing with. Being too young to be taken seriously? Yes. Having enormous shoes to fill in Paul's absence? Certainly. Undoing the evil done by false doctrine? Check. Convincing sinners of the worst kind that Christ died for them? Again, yes. Being selected for this leadership position even though he was naturally timid and unsure of himself, feeling inadequate for the task? Truly.

For Timothy and the Ephesians, Paul established the parameters of his commands and encouragements. Then, no doubt to a sigh of relief from Timothy, Paul launched into specific instructions that he, in his God-given wisdom, knew would bring success.

your notes

For Your Consideration (1:12-20)

1. What advantage was there for Timothy in being reminded at this particular moment of Paul's conversion?

2. Despite his years of service, even being imprisoned for preaching the gospel, Paul referred to himself in the present tense as the worst of sinners. Do you agree with Paul's self-description? What was his motive in describing himself this way?

3. What power does your testimony have to inspire others? How can it change others' opinions of their own abilities?

4. Taking Paul's advice under consideration, what would you do if you ended up being responsible for results you felt hopelessly incapable of achieving?

Chapter 2

The church's worship

Scripture	1 Timothy 2:1-15; 3:14-16

Understanding the theory of a concept or idea is one thing; putting it into practice is another story. There are probably hundreds, maybe thousands, of books about golf. However, you can know all there is to know about the game of golf and still be a terrible golfer. To be successful you have to be able to apply what you know. You have to be able to put theory into practice.

Paul spent the first chapter of 1 Timothy underscoring the importance of the gospel and reminding his young friend that the theory behind his evangelism was to bring believers to love God with a pure heart, good conscience, and a sincere faith. Beginning in chapter 2, Paul switched to an emphasis on how to put that theory into practice. What follows is a concise but thorough handbook on applying the gospel in the real world.

How Christians worship God and how they act during worship defines the gospel to nonbelievers and strengthens it among believers. The gospel is the centerpiece of worship, and Paul launched immediately in the second chapter of 1 Timothy with specific action steps. Though Christians and non-Christians alike may participate in worship, worship is conducted by the faithful not for themselves or the congregation, but for God.

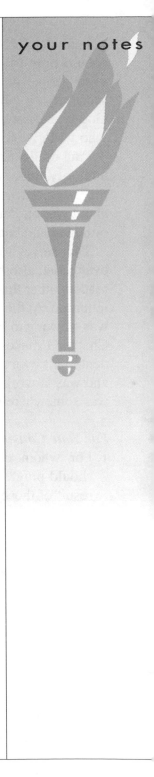

For Your Consideration

1. What are some other places in the Bible where the emphasis is on turning theory into practice?

2. Do you think there's any benefit to understanding the theory of something even if you can't put it into practice or never have the chance to? Why?

3. What kind of situation would prompt you to try to do something before you understood the theory behind it? Are there examples of this in the Bible? (One example from Acts is mentioned in this lesson.)

The Primacy of Prayer (1 Tim. 2:1-7)

First Timothy 2:1-2 lifts up prayer as the source of a "tranquil and quiet life in all godliness and dignity." This is the state God wants for His people. It's a state He makes available to us through prayer in His name.

Prayer holds the highest place in worship because nothing else can place the power of the gospel before the world as prayer can. Have you ever imagined how wonderful it would be to be able to pick up the phone any time of the day or night to get advice from the president or to ask a question to the wisest person alive? That's what prayer is like, only a hundred times better. You have a direct line 24 hours a day to the ultimate Authority, the Creator of all. Pray to Him in sincere humility and you'll get powerful results.

In verse 1 Paul mentioned four prayer types:
- petitions—requests to meet our deepest spiritual needs
- prayers—other requests for our ourselves, made in reverence and humility
- intercessions—requests made on behalf of others
- thanksgivings—expressions of gratitude

Paul delivered specific instructions about whom to pray for. We should pray for everyone (v. 1). Should we really pray for everyone, even people we don't like? Even people who don't deserve it? This seems like a tall order. But after all, we pray because it is pleasing to God (v. 3), not because we see God as some sort of cosmic Santa Claus who will give us something if we ask hard enough.

Paul used a lot of words describing the position of an evangelist as an authority figure (v. 7). He called himself "appointed," "herald," "apostle," and "teacher." Even as he got into the main points of his message about prayer, Paul continued to underscore his position as one who was ordained and equipped to preach the gospel.

This serves to remind all readers of the letter that Timothy, also an evangelist, also had these attributes. We know that Paul was writing for readers other than Timothy, expecting some of the Ephesians to read the letter too. At the same time he was building up Timothy's confidence, he was working to build Timothy's clout and credibility among the citizens. Chapter 1 makes it clear that Timothy was young and not all that confident in his own gifts as an evangelist. Paul hadn't lost sight of those facts and was at work strengthening Timothy's image even as his main focus was somewhere else.

For Your Consideration (2:1-7)

1. For whom did Paul say we should pray? What will be the result of those prayers?

2. Do you believe "kings and all those who are in authority" have special God-given power?

Some cultures and faiths affirm the divine right of kings.

3. How did Paul describe the role of Jesus between God and man?

4. Why do you think Paul interrupted himself in the middle of verse 7 to insist he was telling the truth?

Learning Activity

The Power of Prayer

Complete the definitions of each prayer then list several things for which you can pray right now.

Petitions—requests to meet our _____
-
-
-

Prayers—other requests for our _____, made in _____
-
-
-

Intercessions—requests made _____
-
-
-

Thanksgivings—expressions of _____
-
-
-

List people in authority for whom you can pray—include national and local leaders, church staff, employers, and others.

IN DEPTH

Prayer for America

Believers have a responsibility to pray for political leaders. Prayer pleases God, and America was founded on Christian prayer. The people in power right now may be people you don't support politically. That's all the more reason to pray for God to give them wisdom in protecting our freedoms—the freedom of faith above all.

The Practice of Congregations in Worship (1 Tim. 2:8-15)

Paul delivered specific instructions about how to pray, "lifting up holy hands without anger or argument" (v. 8). This means we shouldn't get caught up in distracting disagreements about worship style; it's the essence that matters. Also in this verse, Paul's instructions to men are different from those he gave to the women, and some of the instructions are likely to raise the eyebrows of a 21st-century reader. But let's take a closer look at what Paul said and why.

Paul gave men and women different instructions because they are different types of people with different responsibilities in the community. It isn't that one is better than another, but one is more capable at specific tasks. Denim isn't the same as silk; but for some purposes denim is better, while for others silk is better. Men and women aren't the same, rather both have their strengths and limitations.

Keep in mind that Timothy faced a wild bunch of churchgoers in Ephesus. We'll learn more about them later, in Paul's Second Letter to Timothy. This cast of characters included men who took advantage of gullible women, and women who spent their days gossiping and their nights flitting from one bed to another.

Paul came down sternly on the women here in part because of the reputation some Ephesian women had earned as followers of the cult of Artemis—the Greek goddess of love—who was widely worshiped by the pagans of the time. His aim was to prevent immoral, careless, or disrespectful behavior in church. He also reminded Timothy that Adam

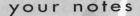

was created first, and that Eve, not Adam, "was deceived and transgressed" in the garden of Eden (vv. 13-14).

Some contemporary commentators jump on Bible passages like this to illustrate what they consider to be the "irrelevance" of Scripture, while others use it as justification for banishing women from any but the most passive role in the affairs of the church. In his excellent study *Be Faithful: 1, 2 Timothy, Titus*, Warren Wiersbe gave a masterful analysis of the issue that cuts to the heart of the truth:

"These days ... the word 'submission' makes some people see red. Some well-meaning writers have even accused Paul of being a 'crusty old bachelor' who was anti-women .... If we have a problem with what the Bible says about women in the church, the issue is not with Paul ... but with the Lord who gave the Word .... Submission is not subjugation. Submission is recognizing God's order in the home and the church, and joyfully obeying it .... Submission is the key to spiritual growth and ministry: Husbands should be submitted to the Lord, Christians should be submitted to each other, and wives should be submitted to the Lord and to their husbands ....

"We must never underestimate the important place that godly women played in the ministry of the church. The Gospel message had a tremendous impact on them, because it affirmed their value before God and their equality in the body of Christ. Women had a low place in the Roman world, but the Gospel changed that.

"'Silence' [2:11] is an unfortunate translation, because it gives the impression that believing women were never to open their mouths in the assembly. This is the same word that is translated "peaceable" ["tranquil" in HCSB®] in verse 2. Some of the women abused their newfound freedom in Christ, and created disturbances in the services by interrupting. It is this problem that Paul addressed in this admonition."[1]

As the *The New American Commentary* explains, "Paul was not demanding physical silence but a teachable spirit."[2]

In Titus—which Paul probably wrote between 1 and 2 Timothy and which along with them is known as the Pastoral Epistles—Paul wrote that women *are* permitted to teach, that older women "are to teach what is good, so that they may encourage the young women" (Titus 2:3-4).

As we learn in 2 Timothy 1:5 and 3:15, Timothy himself was taught at home by his mother and grandmother. And it isn't only other women and children that the Bible instructs women to teach. Acts 18 tells of an Alexandrian Jew named Apollos who arrived in Ephesus. Though he was fervent in the faith, his knowledge was incomplete because "he knew only John's baptism" (Acts 18:25).

The story continues: "He began to speak boldly in the synagogue. After Priscilla and Aquila heard him, they took him home and explained the way of God to him more accurately" (26:27). So women in Ephesus were encouraged to set the record straight by teaching this enthusiastic but misinformed speaker the true and complete story of his Redeemer.

For Your Consideration (2:8-15)

1. How are Paul's instructions about behavior in church different for men and for women?

2. Why did Paul state that a woman should not have authority over a man (v. 12)?

3. How can silence and submission make better Christians?

4. What do you think the difference is between being equal in God's eyes and being the same?

5. How would you relate Paul's instructions for worship to members of your church?

6. Is the way you dress an accurate reflection of the person you are?

7. If Paul were writing his instructions today, what meaning would "modest," "decency," and "good sense" have?

The Mystery of Godliness (1 Tim. 3:14-16)

At the end of chapter 3, Paul expressed the hope that he would be with Timothy in person soon. However, the important thing was not Paul's presence, but the behavior of the Ephesians in church. We saw in 2:8 and following how raucous behavior in the past prompted Paul to set some stringent standards. The worship experience is set apart from the rest of the weekly routine, and behavior should be set apart as well—reverent, humble, and respectful.

The "mystery of godliness" in 3:16 is defined in the words that follow by what many scholars think are the words to an ancient hymn: "God made in human form, preaching the word on earth, being believed, and returning in glory to heaven."

In these closing verses of the chapter, Paul did a remarkable thing by figuratively breaking into song. It's almost as though he couldn't contain his emotion and joy at what he felt as he wrote—words of teaching and encouragement ending with a spontaneous and heartfelt hymn of joy and triumph.

For Your Consideration (3:14-16)
1. How did Paul define the "mystery of godliness"?

2. If you're in charge of a situation but can't be there in person, who's ultimately responsible for the outcome?

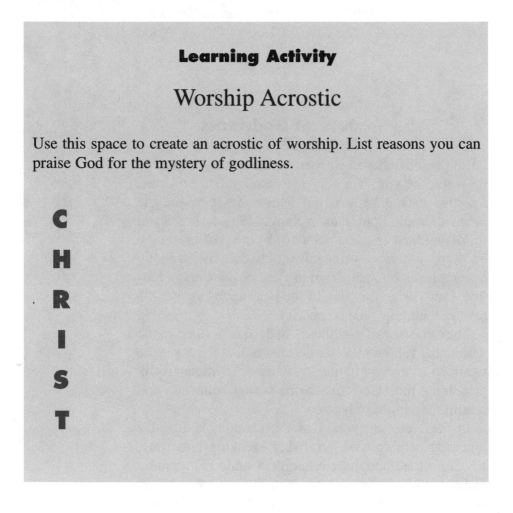

Learning Activity

Worship Acrostic

Use this space to create an acrostic of worship. List reasons you can praise God for the mystery of godliness.

C

H

R

I

S

T

[1]Warren W. Wiersbe, *Be Faithful: 1, 2 Timothy, Titus,* (Wheaton, Illinois: Victor Books, 1981) 34, 36-37. Printed by permission.

[2]Thomas D. Lea and Hayne P. Griffin, Jr., *1,2 Timothy, Titus, The New American Commentary* (Nashville: Broadman Press, 1992), 98.

Chapter

3

The church's Leaders

Scripture	1 Timothy 3:1-13

Think of some outstanding leaders you know. Maybe they're people you've encountered personally. Or they might be political leaders with the weight of great decisions on their shoulders; military leaders whose commands mean the preservation of freedom and life or death to thousands; prominent and successful figures in sports or entertainment. History is filled with the stories of great leaders who made their marks on the world: Alexander the Great, George Washington, Douglas MacArthur.

People become leaders for a variety of reasons. Some set leadership as their goal and do whatever it takes to achieve it. You know the type—they're determined to be in charge from the time they can walk. Others display a natural gift of leadership that lifts them up above their peers. Still others step into a situation where there's no leader at all and—to their own surprise—rise to the challenge.

In 1 Timothy 3, Paul explained in detail what kind of people should lead the Christian church. We'll see that the apostle made his point in two ways: first, by what he said; and second, by what he left out.

This was a time in church history when the original leaders of Christianity were gradually fading from the scene and the church needed new leaders to take their places. Throughout chapter 3 Paul described the character, commitment, and heart of church leaders. But he said little about exactly what they're supposed to do. Clearly Paul's experience taught him that character is more important in a leader than accomplishments. If the right character is there, the accomplishments will follow.

Our history is filled with people who did heroic things, but whose positions as leaders were destroyed by ungodly character. One example in recent years was the downfall of President Richard Nixon. He was a man of great intellect, blessed with many leadership qualities, and his accomplishments were historic: ending the Vietnam War, establishing political ties with Communist China, and promoting nuclear disarmament talks with the Soviet Union. Yet his career ended in disgrace as he became the only American president in history to resign from office. Because he used dishonest means to achieve his goals, he ultimately failed as a leader.

Time and again history teaches us the lesson that corrupt leaders, no matter how brilliant they are, are destined ultimately to fail because great accomplishments can never last when they're built on a foundation of lies and deceit. On the other hand, people who seem to be completely average can become effective leaders under the right circumstances. Timothy was evidently a normal, unremarkable young man to begin with. But the Lord equipped him to preach and proclaim the gospel, then gave him the opportunity to represent Paul's ministry to the Ephesians.

Paul made it clear to Timothy that the end never justifies the means. In any leadership position, and especially as leaders in the church, the people in charge must be mature, godly, and beyond reproach.

For Your Consideration
1. Who do you think are the greatest leaders of our time? What makes them great?

2. What characteristics do you think all great church leaders have in common?

3. What's the biggest challenge leaders must overcome? What special challenges exist for leaders in your church?

Requirements for Church Elders
(1 Tim. 3:1-7)

Some leaders are charismatic and love the spotlight, while others prefer to work behind the scenes. Paul affirmed that style isn't important but substance is. First of all the apostle said that becoming a leader is a noble act (1 Tim. 3:1). True leaders are selfless and place their responsibility to the people ahead of anything else.

Then Paul followed with a list of specific character traits. A leader must be "above reproach, the husband

Learning Activity

Husband of One Wife

In both lists of qualifications, Paul stated that leaders must be husbands of one wife (1 Tim. 3:2,12). Why do you think this qualification is so important that it is on both lists?

of one wife, self-controlled, sensible, respectable, hospitable, an able teacher, not addicted to wine, not a bully but gentle, not quarrelsome, not greedy—one who manages his own household competently, having his children under control with all dignity" (vv. 2b-5).

The word for *overseer* in verse 1 can also be translated *bishop* or *elder*. Each of these last two has a specific meaning in some present-day denominations, but in Paul's context all three words are interchangeable.

There's a lot of discussion in the church today about what "the husband of one wife" (v. 2) actually means. It doesn't exclude single men from positions of leadership; if it did, Paul himself would have been excluded! Widowers or never married men surely can serve as elders. Some interpreters believe Paul was forbidding divorced men from serving as church leaders; others believe the apostle was demanding that the church leader be faithful to his one wife. If a church member can't stick to biblical principles in his own life, he's not likely to be able to teach those principles to others.

Another noteworthy requirement is that an elder not be "greedy" (v. 3), which is to say Christian leaders—or any Christian for that matter—should never be obsessed with money or love money so that it controls him or her. There's nothing in the Bible that says Christians can't be rich, but money should never be a god or a driving force to them. Money

Getty Images

Though wealth by itself is no sin, money brings power and responsibility that Christians are called to use for the good of the church.

your notes

is a powerful force in the world, and like any force it can work for good or for evil.

Continuing with his list of character issues, Paul made it clear that just meeting the basic requirements wasn't good enough. The more troubled the past history of an organization is, the more scrupulous the moral standards of a new leader must be. Think of a situation you know about where a business or organization was completely corrupt. Finally the forces of reform took over, threw the rotten leadership out, and installed new blood dedicated to steering a morally upright course. However, to regain the respect of people both inside and outside the organization, the new leaders can't be just decent, law-abiding citizens. They must hold themselves to far higher moral and ethical standards than normal in order to make it clear that the company is making a new start.

This was the case in the Roman Empire during the time of Paul and Timothy. First-century Rome was one of the most corrupt and immoral cultures in the history of the world. Leaders of the church couldn't be just reasonably decent folks. They had to hold to the highest possible moral standards to set themselves clearly apart from the culture. (Paul gave comparable qualifications for elders or overseers in Titus 1:5-9, which was probably written between the two letters to Timothy.)

The church, both then and today, must have fully mature Christian leaders in order to help the church mature.

For Your Consideration (3:1-7)

1. What is the first requirement of a church leader? Why is that requirement listed first?

2. Why shouldn't a new convert be an elder?

3. What's the best way to avoid becoming "addicted to wine"?

4. How is this whole passage a compliment to Timothy?

Requirements for Church Deacons
(1 Tim. 3:8-10,12-13)

Unless it is extremely small, every organization has more than one leader; it has a hierarchy of leaders. After describing in detail what kind of man an elder of the church should be, Paul went on to list the requirements for a deacon. *Deacon* comes from the Greek word *diakonos*,

Learning Activity

Character Matters

In the space provided, write a poem, create an acrostic, or simply describe why character is an important trait for church leaders. Include thoughts or ideas that communicate what that character should include.

IN DEPTH

Titus 1:5-9

Titus was preaching and teaching in Crete, doing much the same work there that Timothy was doing in Ephesus, and Paul wrote him a similar letter of encouragement. Note both the similarities and the differences between the requirements for church leaders in the two places. There are constant standards, but Paul modified the details to meet the needs of specific congregations:

"The reason I left you in Crete was to set right what was left undone and, as I directed you, to appoint elders in every town, someone who is blameless, the husband of one wife, having faithful children not accused of wildness or rebellion. For an overseer, as God's manager, must be blameless, not arrogant, not quick tempered, not addicted to wine, not a bully, not greedy for money, but hospitable, loving what is good, sensible, righteous, holy, self-controlled, holding to the faithful message as taught, that he will be able both to encourage with sound teaching and to refute those who contradict it."

which literally means *servant*. The first deacons were mentioned in Acts 6, when the original apostles heard complaints that certain widows were being slighted by not getting the assistance from the church that others received. Rather than spend time away from teaching and preaching, the apostles asked other believers to take on the responsibility.

Today a deacon is usually one who serves by taking on the day-to-day responsibilities of running a church so that the elders can concentrate on teaching and spiritual development. Reading through these verses, you'll see that the men described are much like the elders Paul described in the previous verses. Many characteristics are identical: worthy of respect, not a drunkard, not greedy, the husband of one wife, and in control of their children and household.

First Timothy 3:9 is noteworthy: "holding the mystery of the faith with a clear conscience." Up to this point, Paul for the most part had told Timothy specific things a deacon should not be. Now here's a positive demand rather than a negative one. This "mystery of the faith" is the teaching once hidden in darkness but now revealed by the power of the risen Lord. Faith, as *The New American Commentary* explains, is "the content of the Christian religion. It is objective Christian truth."[1]

For Your Consideration (3:8-10,12-13)

1. What are the similarities and differences between the qualifications for elders and deacons?

2. If the descriptions of elders and deacons are so nearly the same, why have two lists?

3. How can serving as a deacon change somebody both in human eyes and in God's?

4. How has the definition of "having your children under control" changed over time? Is this change good or bad?

Requirements for Women in the Church
(1 Tim. 3:11)

Paul gave women special attention here, as he did in 1 Timothy 2:9-15, because he knew the importance of women in increasing both the depth and the reach of Christianity. Some translations use the word *woman* in this verse, but since the verses on both sides of this one are talking about deacons, the context almost certainly means Paul was talking about the wives of deacons here, and not women in general. As we've seen, women have an essential role in the work of the church, and Paul singled out the helpmeets of church leaders, declaring they must "be worthy of respect, not slanderers, self-controlled, faithful in everything" (3:11).

Remember that in our last lesson we discussed the fact that Ephesian women were known for their flashy way of dressing and gossiping; Paul was determined to preempt that kind of behavior in the church by his instructions for them to "learn in silence" (2:11). Here too he admonished them not to slander and to show self-control. Reverent and respectful, women can lead through their own example.

Elders, deacons, and women all have important and distinctive functions in the church. Paul emphasized the need for each group to participate in the life of the church by mentioning them separately. He also re-emphasized the basic truth that character is more important than accomplishment by showing that, whatever your position or task, the moral requirements are very nearly the same.

For Your Consideration (3:11)

1. How are the requirements for women different from requirements for other church leaders? Why?

2. What are some examples of work women can do for the church that men can't?

3. What women played a special and unique role in Timothy's life?

---

[1]Thomas D. Lea and Hayne P. Griffin, Jr., *1,2 Timothy, Titus, The New American Commentary* (Nashville: Broadman Press, 1992), 117.

Chapter 4

The church and its Doctrine

Scripture	1 Timothy 4:1-16

W hat is truth? It sounds like such a simple and straightforward question, but coming up with the answer is one of the most important responsibilities you will ever face as a Christian.

There was a time not too long ago when this question would have been completely unnecessary. Everybody knew what truth was, and our public institutions proudly and predictably upheld it. Truth was a time-tested, absolute value everybody recognized and agreed on. Regardless of where you lived or what you were doing, the standard was universal.

Today, however, the whole idea of truth is under attack. Absolute truth, the idea that there is one truth for everybody in every situation, has been replaced in the popular culture by relative truth.

You run up against relative truth all the time. Chances are if you haven't encountered it yet today, you will before bedtime. "Well, that's fine for you, but don't impose your standards on me!" is one common expression of the idea. "If it feels good, do it" is another.

The trouble is that relative standards are no standards at all. What if the next time someone said, "If it feels good, do it," another person nearby poured a glass of water over his head? He'd sputter with shock, anger, and embarrassment, and then say, "Why in the world did you do that?"

Relative truth leads not to freedom, but to anarchy.

Getty Images

"Well," the other might answer, "you said 'If it feels good, do it' and pouring water on your head felt good to me."

Remember that the lack of absolute truth (and other absolutes, for that matter) isn't freedom; it's anarchy. If truth were really relative, people could commit robbery, murder, or any other act without punishment. In a relative world there can be no laws.

We're not an anarchy yet, though there are many misguided people who think having no rules would be wonderful. But we are dangerously relativistic. And in a relativistic world, the church is the rock of truth. There is no greater commitment for a Christian leader than to maintain sound Christian doctrine.

The more relativistic the culture, the more important the church's function is to hold fast to and uplift the truth. In Ephesus during the time of Paul and Timothy, hypocrites and liars threatened the truth and the teachings of the church. In the fourth chapter of 1 Timothy, Paul emphasized the importance of holding fast to the truth and gave Timothy encouragement that he had been equipped by God to be a truth teller.

For Your Consideration
1. What is truth? Is everybody's definition the same?

2. What kind of society would we have if everybody defined truth individually?

Defending God's Truth (1 Tim. 4:1-5)

Timothy's responsibility was to make sure the Ephesians knew what the truth looked like. Paul wasn't surprised at the power and variety of false teachings. He reminded Timothy of the certainty of "deceitful spirits and the teachings of demons" (v. 1) and "the hypocrisy of liars whose consciences are seared" (v. 2). The message to Timothy—and to today's church leaders—was that he was entrusted by God with the task of upholding the truth.

Verse 1 is the only place in the Pastoral Epistles that mentions demons. We don't typically think of demonic influences coming from within the church, but it can happen. In fact, Matthew 16 describes how Satan used Peter to tempt Jesus: "Then Peter took Him aside and began to rebuke Him, 'Oh no, Lord! This will never happen to You!' But He turned and told Peter, 'Get behind Me, Satan! You are an offense to Me, because you're not thinking about God's concerns, but man's'" (Matt. 16:22-23).

Learning Activity

False Focus

Paul listed four characteristics of those who depart from the faith.

1. The teaching they follow is _____.

2. They are _____ _____.

3. They wrongfully abstain from _____ and _____.

4. They have an obsession with _____ _____

_____.

This also reflects Jesus' teaching that false prophets would rise up: "For false messiahs and false prophets will rise up and will perform signs and wonders to lead astray, if possible, the elect" (Mark 13:22).

In 1 Timothy 4:3, Paul recounted some of the untruths proclaimed against Christian teaching. These self-appointed experts in God's law were actually spouting laws of their own. These weren't absolute laws, but the laws of individuals obsessed with calling the shots and maintaining control. But the real truth—the absolute truth—is God's truth, "sanctified by the word of God and by prayer" (v. 5).

For Your Consideration (4:1-5)
1. What examples did Paul give of the types of lies false teachers were telling?

2. Why should nothing created by God be rejected by man?

3. What effect do hypocritical church members have on the effectiveness of the church?

Godliness Is Good Forever (1 Tim. 4:6-10)

A godly leader must know and speak the truth. Pointing out the absolute truth, said Paul, is a way to be "a good servant of Christ Jesus" (v. 6). Again he warned Timothy not to get caught up in false doctrine but to be spiritually nurtured by faith and truthful teaching.

In the face of worldly falsehoods, godliness is the best personal goal you can set. Everything else is temporary. This reminder in verse 8 was surely important for Timothy, and it's equally important in contemporary

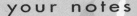

your notes

culture. Everywhere you glance—on television, in the news magazines, on the movie screens—the message is blasted out that looks are everything. Youth, beauty, sexy clothes, expensive cars, and desirable companions are the most important things in the world.

We obsess about our appearance and our taste in fashion. We spend money we don't have for things we don't need, but that our culture has convinced us we do need. A more complex society offers more complex enticements than in Timothy's time, but the message is the same. Do this, look this way, and you'll be happy and fulfilled.

Christians should know better. All the world's enticements are temporary and ultimately worthless. But godliness enhances every aspect of a person's character, and the effect isn't short-term. It lasts a lifetime, and then for eternity beyond a lifetime. Don't worry about perfect images or making a perfect impression; worry about perfect truth.

When Paul wrote that God is "the Savior of all men," he didn't mean that everybody will be saved whether they want to be or not. Rather, any sinner can be saved by God's grace even though not one of us deserves to be rescued from the wrath of the Lord.

Stay the course. Keep away from foolish untruths. Godliness is the best personal goal you can set because it lasts forever. Put hope in the only thing that matters: the living and eternal God.

For Your Consideration (4:6-10)

1. How does Jesus spiritually nourish His leaders?

2. What makes godliness better than physical strength or beauty?

3. Why do you think Paul made it a point to warn Timothy away from "irreverent and silly myths"?

4. How can church members today nourish and encourage their leaders?

5. What are some present-day examples of making "the training of the body" more important than godliness?

IN DEPTH

Christ the Savior

Outside the New Testament the Greek word *soter*, meaning "savior" or "deliverer," was used to describe deserving men, leading officials, rulers, and deities. The term implied the person was a protector or deliverer and it was used to describe Roman emperors. But in the New Testament, *soter* is used exclusively to refer to Jesus Christ and to God the Father. As Savior, Christ grants forgiveness, protects, and saves His people from death. He is the Savior of those who believe and call on Him (1 Tim. 4:10).

Gaining Confidence (1 Tim. 4:11-16)

It's well established that Timothy was young and inexperienced. Here again, as earlier in the chapter, Paul encouraged him not to be distracted or discouraged by his youth. "No one should despise your youth," Paul reminded him in verse 12. Instead, Timothy had the God-given gifts to stand out as a teacher and leader. His exemplary conduct could overcome any perception that he didn't have the experience to carry out his ministry.

Even so, Paul advised Timothy not to be satisfied with his abilities as a teacher but to practice and improve them. By doing so he would be teaching the people as well as honing the skills that would improve his effectiveness in the future.

Christian maturity has nothing to do with chronological age. We have the example of Jesus talking with the temple elders when He was only 12. Billy Graham was an ordained minister at 21, and only 10 years later he was holding his first crusade.

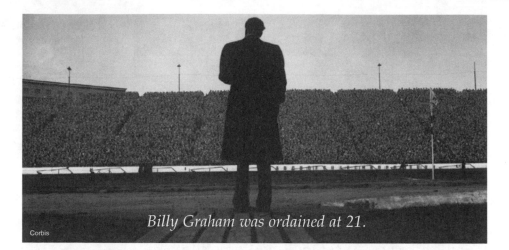

Billy Graham was ordained at 21.

Corbis

Pastoring is a supernatural gift and calling; it can be given early or late in life, as God chooses. It isn't an internal or private calling, but an exhortation to speak out and stand up for the gospel in a public setting. Though Timothy may have had doubts about his ability to preach and lead at so young an age, he didn't doubt his calling. Neither did Paul. In fact, Paul's confidence in Timothy's gift prompted him to keep encouraging Timothy to make the most of it.

Every pastor I know vividly remembers the moment he was called to preach. My call took place on our farm in Appomattox, Virginia, on a cold January night. I was in bed in my room listening to the radio and watching the snow falling outside. There, in that otherwise unremarkable time and place, I clearly heard the Sovereign God speak to me the unmistakable word that I would preach. I didn't know what my skills were then, whether I would be a good preacher or a lousy one. What I knew was that I would follow the Lord wherever He would lead me. It was an open-ended call and I was willing to go anywhere, praying in faith that God would give me whatever skills I needed for the challenges ahead.

Maybe you've been in a situation where you promised to work toward some goal without knowing exactly what skills you'd need when you got there, or whether you could get them. At the end of chapter 4, Timothy was reminded that he had a special gift from God that was recognized by the church elders (v. 14). He was to rise above any perceived shortcomings and reach up to the One who gave him the power to teach in Christ's name.

God selects people to lead His church then through faith equips them to be leaders. God's leaders seldom question the fact that they're called to lead, but often question their own qualifications. Just as God inspired Paul to encourage Timothy, He inspires us to encourage our leaders. They have a difficult and sometimes lonely job. Our job is to lift them up in the name of the Lord.

For Your Consideration (4:11-16)

1. What kind of example should Timothy have set when he preached?

Learning Activity

Fitness Record

For the next week, keep track of how much time you spend working on your physical fitness (diet, exercise, and so on). In the second column, keep track of how much time you spend on your spiritual fitness (worship, daily time alone with God, prayer, and so on).

Physical		Spiritual	
Monday	_____	Monday	_____
Tuesday	_____	Tuesday	_____
Wednesday	_____	Wednesday	_____
Thursday	_____	Thursday	_____
Friday	_____	Friday	_____
Saturday	_____	Saturday	_____
Sunday	_____	Sunday	_____

2. Why should Timothy keep practicing his preaching and public reading?

3. Why did Paul keep bringing up Timothy's age?

4. What are some other examples of young people doing great works for the Lord?

5. Would it be hard to be an authority figure at a young age? What are some of the problems? How could you overcome them?

IN DEPTH

Billy Graham

Corbis

As a young evangelist, Billy Graham might well have felt some of the same uncertainty Timothy did. Like Timothy, Graham questioned his fitness for the ministry but never the fact that he was called to preach and teach in the name of the Lord. After graduating from Wheaton College and serving as a church pastor in Illinois for a few years, Graham staged his first ever crusade in Los Angeles in 1949. It was a big, busy city with lots of distractions. It was during the middle of the Southern California summer and the services were held inside a stifling hot tent. But Graham and his team didn't concentrate on the obstacles to their ministry. They concentrated instead on making the most of the gifts God gave them. What was supposed to be a week-long crusade lasted three months, and Graham was on his way to being the leading evangelist of the century.

Chapter

5

The church and its members

| Scripture | 1 Timothy 5:1–6:2 |

We think of the church first of all as a place to learn about the Bible and how to apply its teachings in our lives. But consider how important the church today has become as a center of social interaction. There are youth groups, seniors organizations, mission trips, Sunday School picnics, Wednesday night suppers—an almost endless list of opportunities to mix with other members and visitors.

Church is a *community* of believers working together in the name of Christ. There's more than just the relationship between you and Christ going on—there also are the relationships between you and everyone else worshiping with you. Every relationship nurtured by the church represents a chance for you to multiply your ministry and extend your reach to the world for the cause of Christ.

This is the point Paul made at the end of his first letter to his young evangelist friend Timothy. He underscored the importance of social relationships in the church and highlighted the differences among different types of believers. Maintaining these proper relationships within the church gives members of all types the best opportunities possible for serving others in the name of Christ and for multiplying their ministries.

For Your Consideration

1. How do social activities affect your attitude toward your church?

2. How do church social activities enhance outreach to your community?

3. What are the liabilities to having a church with a busy social schedule?

A Family of Believers (1 Tim. 5:1-2)

Paul began by explaining the importance of treating people according to their age and gender. When you were little, did your parents tell you to "respect your elders"? That meant being polite and courteous, honoring their age and experience. Even if they're in error, old people deserve respect. Of course Timothy needed to take Paul's advice himself; he was probably younger than most of the people he preached to.

Timothy was to respect older men as his fathers and younger men as his brothers. In similar fashion, Paul instructed Timothy to revere the older women as mothers and the younger ones as sisters. If Timothy expected to make any headway as an evangelist, he had to earn the respect of his audience; they must feel personally comfortable with him.

For Your Consideration (5:1-2)

1. Why did Paul single out specific ages and genders when describing how we should treat each other?

2. How have attitudes toward the treatment of older people and women changed in recent years? Are the changes good or bad?

Widows with Children (1 Tim. 5:3-4)

Don't you wish you could help everybody who needed help? These days we're besieged by an incredible variety of people representing a cause or a need. Many of them appear to be legitimate and sincere. But even if they all were sincere and you sympathized with every cause, you couldn't help everybody.

At some point every person and every church has limits on its resources. Paul told Timothy how to discern whether a widow was in severe enough need to merit drawing on the church's modest resources. Two conditions must be met: first, they must have no relatives to take care of them. If they do have relatives, it's the relatives' responsibility—not the church's—to provide for them. The nuclear family has the first responsibility, and if there is no such family, then the church family is next in line. This care ties in with the respect Paul said must be shown to older people, which many widows were.

your notes

Learning Activity

Community Affirmation

Below, list the names of those within your church community to whom you could minister in the weeks to come. Using the suggested ideas, or others that you identify, plan to minister to others through acts of ministry or through expressions of affirmation.

Names: _____

_____

_____

_____

__ letter	__ card
__ e-mail	__ phone call
__ deliver a small gift	__ run an errand
__ service ministry	__ baked goods
__ gift certificates	__ other:_____

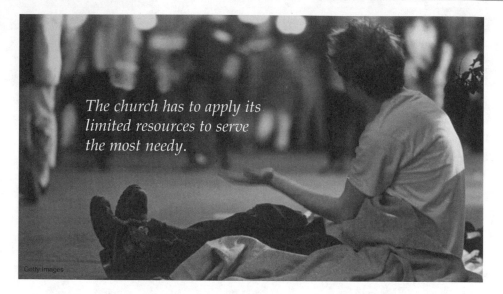

The church has to apply its limited resources to serve the most needy.

Paul's specific instruction was to "support" widows (v. 3). This included financial assistance but certainly included more than that—companionship, encouragement, prayer, and other nonmonetary expressions of help.

For Your Consideration (5:3-4)
1. What kind of people did Paul consider to be "genuinely widows"?

2. What is the responsibility of the children and grandchildren of widows?

3. How can you separate the truly needy from everyone else asking for help? What standards should you use?

Widows Without Children (1 Tim. 5:5-11)
A widow without children or grandchildren is the one Paul called the "real widow" (v. 5). The church is obliged to care for the widow who is "left all alone, has put her hope in God and continues night and day in her petitions and prayers" (v. 5). Furthermore, a widow worthy of support by the church is one who lives within her means. She is not to be "self-indulgent" as the *Holman Christian Standard Bible*® says. The *New*

International Version uses "lives for pleasure" (v. 6). The original Greek word here is found only one other place in the New Testament and has the connotation of "luxurious, voluptuous indulgence." A woman who lives in that manner can scarcely have her eyes on serving the Lord. Moreover, she creates an unnecessary burden on the church by living an expensive lifestyle and expecting others to pay for it.

In verse 8 Paul reminded his readers that Christians must live by a higher standard than others do. What might be acceptable behavior for nonbelievers is unacceptable for followers of Christ. Every day as a Christian you'll run into situations you would handle differently if you were a non-Christian. Other people, Christian and non-Christian alike, have higher expectations of you. Then, as now, members of Christ's church must set the bar higher for themselves in matters of moral judgment.

Paul's first qualification for widows on the "official support list" (v. 9) was that they be "at least 60 years old." This is not to say widows under that age weren't eligible for support under any circumstances. But it was assumed that a woman younger than 60 would be able to earn a living on her own and might even remarry. On the other hand, neither does it mean all widows in a congregation should expect to be totally supported by the members from their 60th birthday on. Two other requirements were that they be the wife of one husband and that they be known for good works.

Paul was saying that the church should ensure that the widows among them live comfortable, dignified lives without worrying about food, shelter, and other basics. Today there are a host of government and private insurance programs to give widows financial security. Those who have such help should not look to the church for money. After using their own resources, they should expect help from children and grandchildren. Only after those sources are emptied should they

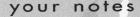

be supported by the church—but then the church should do so willingly and generously. And remember that "support" means more than money. Churches are called to bring companionship and encouragement to widows regardless of their financial status.

For Your Consideration (5:5-11)

1. What are the characteristics of a widow worthy of support by the church?

2. According to Paul, how old should a widow be to qualify for church assistance? What other specific requirements did Paul mention?

3. How relevant are Paul's criteria today?

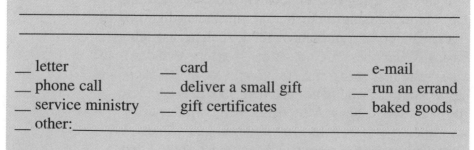

Learning Activity

Pastor/Church Staff Appreciation

Below, list the names of your pastor and other church staff members. Using the suggested ideas, or others that you identify, plan to minister and show appreciation to your pastor and other church staff through acts of ministry or through expressions of affirmation.

Names: _____

_____

_____

__ letter   __ card   __ e-mail
__ phone call   __ deliver a small gift   __ run an errand
__ service ministry   __ gift certificates   __ baked goods
__ other:_____

4. What is the Christian response to a widow who needs help only because she insists on living beyond her means?

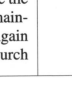

IN DEPTH

The Value of Friendship

Giving support to widows or others in need involves more than money, though financial assistance is often the most obvious way to help. Widows are frequently lonely. Companionship and conversation can mean the world to someone whose husband and family are gone. A card or phone call are welcome signs of interest and encouragement as well. Such expressions let them know someone cares and gives them the chance to experience the love of Christ through you.

Caution to Young Widows (1 Tim. 5:12-16)

When you get something without having to work for it, you never appreciate it as much as if you had to make some sort of sacrifice or effort. Paul instructed Timothy not to enroll young widows on the official list for assistance because he was convinced it would make them idle gossips. They hadn't lived as long or learned as much as the older widows; making their condition too easy was something the church in Ephesus should avoid.

Paul wanted young widows to remarry, "have children, manage their households, and give the adversary no opportunity to accuse us" (v. 14). Churches have the obligation to contribute to a truly needy widow's maintenance, but not to a young widow's idleness. Again Paul was thinking of how the young Ephesian church could best use its limited resources. No doubt if a young widow in special circumstances had a genuine need, he would instruct the church to meet it.

For Your Consideration (5:12-16)

1. According to Paul, why should the church not give assistance to young widows?

2. Do you believe the Lord helps those who help themselves? How does that saying apply here?

Treatment of Church Leaders (1 Tim. 5:17-25)

Now Paul moved on to the treatment of church leaders. He already had written about the need to assist worthy widows financially. Here he instructed the church to pay their "elders" who were "good leaders" an "ample honorarium" for their work (v. 17). The literal Greek description of their payment is "double honor," possibly referring to both respect and financial compensation, or possibly to a double portion of salary. Paul quoted Jesus' statement that the "laborer is worthy of his pay" (Matt. 10:10; Luke 10:7). Elders and other church leaders need to spend their time teaching, preaching, evangelizing, and studying. That's a full-time job if done responsibly. Make it possible for these people to answer their calling to share the gospel without having to worry about their daily bread.

Pastors are fallible human beings and subject to sin and temptation. An empty accusation, however, should never be enough to condemn someone. There should be evidence from "two or three witnesses" (v. 19). The experience of being falsely accused is a helpless, unfair feeling. If you're a church leader, such a false accusation can render you untrustworthy in the eyes of the people you're trying to reach. Propriety and honesty are essential, but a man's reputation must not be unfairly compromised, as that will also compromise his ability to preach effectively.

Like a concerned father, Paul warned Timothy not to "share in the sins of others" (v. 22), which we would call "running with the wrong crowd." A church leader must always be aware that he is setting an example.

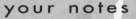

For Your Consideration (5:17-25)

1. How should church leaders be compensated for their work?

2. Are today's church leaders held to higher standards of behavior than everybody else? Should they be?

Slaves and Masters (1 Tim. 6:1-2)

Slavery was common in biblical times, though it was not usually the same kind of slavery associated with colonial America. America and other parts of the British Empire practiced chattel slavery, in which a slave was his owner's property just like a horse or a table. Biblical slaves were often indentured servants working off their apprenticeships, prisoners of war who were eventually exchanged, criminals serving a sentence, or people who sold themselves into slavery for a specific period to pay a debt.

Christianity in Timothy's time was having a transforming effect on the institution of slavery. The influence of Christianity gave masters a sense of accountability to God for the way they treated slaves, and it gave slaves an eternal incentive to be obedient. Even so, Paul treaded lightly here. He cautioned slaves to be respectful, particularly if they had "believing masters" (v. 2). The New Testament consistently instructs Christians to be servants. Here Paul used the mirror image of servants (or slaves) behaving in a way pleasing to Christ.

For Your Consideration (6:1-2)

1. How should slaves treat their masters?

2. How did Christianity transform the institution of slavery?

6

The church and its priorities

Scripture	1 Timothy 6:3-21

It's a sad sign of the times to hear about incredibly rich people who lied, cheated, and stole over the years to maintain their wealth or to become even richer. When the economic boom of the 1990s came to an end, these people could have lived lavishly on what they already had; they had been earning more every year than most of us will make in a lifetime. But what they had—the huge estates, the yachts, the million-dollar paintings—wasn't enough for them. So they broke the law, robbing innocent employees and stockholders of hundreds of millions of dollars, destroying companies, putting thousands out of work, and eventually trading their millionaire mansions for prison cells.

No matter how much they had, it was never enough. Like so many people in our culture, they were trying to buy happiness and contentment because they didn't know any other way to get them. As old and familiar as the idea is, when it comes right down to it, too many people fail to realize that you can't buy happiness at any price.

There was a feature article in a newspaper not long ago about a couple who had lived on the same farm for more than 40 years. They didn't have much in the way of worldly things, but what they had was paid for. In the picture accompanying the article, the two of them were sitting under a shade tree shelling peas into a pan. He wore overalls and she had

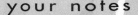

on a plain cotton work dress. They were talking and smiling, passing the time on a beautiful summer afternoon. From a material standpoint they might not have had much to show for a lifetime of work, just a house on a few acres, a car, a tractor, and maybe a few thousand dollars in the bank. Yet they had a degree of contentment that a hundred million dollars couldn't buy.

The desire to make money and the desire to be happy are two driving forces of modern life. The danger is in believing the first will get you the second and if you have enough material wealth, you'll be content. The falsehood of this assumption is clearly revealed to us every day. At the conclusion of his First Letter of Timothy, Paul pointed out the dangers of concentrating on material wealth and reminded Timothy of the only reliable source of true contentment.

For Your Consideration

1. Why do some rich people seem so unhappy and miserable, while some of modest means seem fully content and satisfied?

2. How would you define "rich"?

3. What differences would there be between the dangers of wealth in Paul's time and today?

The Greed of False Teaching
(1 Tim. 6:3-8)

You don't have to be rich to be content, but you do have to know the truth. People who insist on distorting the truth for their own selfish purposes will always be a threat to godly men and women. These people will always be unfulfilled. In verses 3-5, Paul briefly but clearly described how ruin evolves from falsehood.

By itself, money is neither good nor evil.

PhotoDisc

Teaching doctrine that goes against the "sound teaching of our Lord Jesus Christ" is the work of a "conceited" man with a "sick interest" in arguments (vv. 3-4). This leads to a list of dismal and sinful characteristics including "envy, quarreling, slanders, evil suspicions, and constant disagreement" (vv. 4-5) among men who see godliness only as a pathway to riches. Twisting the truth and using Christianity as a means of self-enrichment leads to disaster.

Though godliness in pursuit of wealth will fail, "godliness with contentment is a great gain" (v. 6). Keep that thought in mind as you imagine what it will take to make you content. Denying the truth of Christ has profound consequences, while recognizing Him as the way, the truth, and the life yields blessings beyond measure.

Unfortunately, some false teachers have found large followings by preaching a "name it and claim it" message that God wants everybody to be rich in material things. These preachers of prosperity will always attract a following, but they lead in the wrong direction—toward a quest for riches rather than contentment in Christ. God promises He will provide for our daily needs. Insisting on more is nothing but covetousness.

For Your Consideration (6:3-8)

1. What words describe someone who teaches false doctrine?

2. What problems come from false doctrine?

Learning Activity

Godliness

Using the letters of "godliness," develop an acrostic that describes godliness or lists some of the characteristics that lead to godliness.

G
O
D
L
I
N
E
S
S

3. What makes false teachers so popular?

4. Who are some false teachers of the present day? What evidence is there to show how dangerous they are?

IN DEPTH

Preach God, Not Riches

In every Christian era including our own, false preachers have emerged who promise an easy path to riches. "Name it," they say, and then "claim it" because God wants you to have it: an expensive new car, fancy clothes, a big house in an exclusive neighborhood. It's easy to attract a following by promising easy riches. But Jesus never promised any of His followers material wealth. In fact, He told His followers that they would be forced to suffer for His sake. Dedicated Christians are much more likely to lose worldly riches than to gain them. But the reward is worth more than all the treasure the world can offer: eternal life.

Temptation Versus Faith
(1 Tim. 6:9-12)

This section of Paul's letter contains one of the most often quoted verses in the Bible. Even non-Christians are familiar with the first phrase of verse 10: "For the love of money is a root of all kinds of evil." Some translations have "the love of money is the root of all evil." This is not only one of the most familiar verses in Scripture, but also one of the most misunderstood.

In verse 9 Paul cautioned about the temptations that come as a result of the desire for wealth. Our fallen nature makes money a tempting goal. When we give in to temptation, the result is "ruin and destruction" (v. 9). What's important to notice, however, is Paul was not saying money is bad, or that Christians shouldn't be rich. There's nothing wrong with money, but the love of money brings evil in the long run.

Corbis

Andrew Carnegie's philanthropy is still benefiting tens of thousands of people a year.

Money on its own can be a wonderful tool for good. After the early 20th century philanthropist Andrew Carnegie sold his steel empire, he gave millions of dollars away to charitable causes, including money for the purchase of thousands of church organs all across the United States. Today, private families and foundations give hundreds of millions of dollars around the world every year for medical research, famine relief, education, and Christian outreach. In theory at least, the more money Christians have the more money the church has in tithes and offerings to spread the news of Christ in the world.

When people with money have the right attitude and perspective, their money becomes a good thing in the world. But when the temptation to be rich drives people to evil, they will soon find they have "wandered away from the faith and pierced themselves with many pains" (v. 10).

In the next two verses Paul gave Timothy both a warning and a challenge. Paul told Timothy to run from the greed and temptation he had just been writing about and also to pursue the worthy attributes of "righteousness, godliness, faith, love, endurance, and gentleness" (v. 11).

Paul went on, part gentle grandfather and part coach in the locker room at halftime: "Fight the good fight

Learning Activity

Pursue These Things

righteousness—

godliness—

faith—

love—

endurance—

gentleness—

for the faith; take hold of eternal life, to which you were called and have made a good confession before many witnesses" (v. 12).

Paul called Timothy a "man of God" in this passage (v. 11), one of only two uses of this title in the New Testament. (The other is in 2 Timothy 3:17.) It is a strong term with a long tradition dating back to Moses, Samuel, and Elisha. It was a powerful reminder to Timothy, and to us, that no one who serves the Lord as a pastor preaches or leads on his own. He is there as God's representative to do His work, above worldly ambitions or temptations.

This list of attributes or goals is an important reminder that godliness is much more than going to church or associating ourselves with church affairs. Godliness extends into every aspect of life, every response to the opportunities and challenges of the world, and every relationship. These are the priorities of true Christians.

For Your Consideration (6:9-12)

1. What does the pursuit of riches lead to?

2. Is money the cause of all evil?

3. Restate 1 Timothy 6:10 in your own words. Why do you think this verse has been so misunderstood?

4. If you could suddenly pay off all your debts and have a million dollars left over, what would you do with it? (Be truthful!)

IN DEPTH

Andrew Carnegie

Moving to the United States from his native Scotland as a boy, Andrew Carnegie took a job in a cotton mill at $1.20 a week. At 16 he went to work for the Pennsylvania Railroad, then invested in the steel industry. At 33 his income was $50,000 a year, and by 1900, the year he turned 65, he made $25 million annually. He established funds to build more than 2,500 public libraries around the world, support retired professors, promote world peace, underwrite scientific research, and help purchase more than 7,500 organs for churches across America.

Waiting on the Lord, Guarding His Word (1 Tim. 6:13-21)

Paul charged Timothy "to keep the commandment without spot or blame until the appearing of our Lord Jesus Christ" (v. 14), having faith that He will return in

His own perfect time. When Paul wrote of the "appearing" of Christ, he used *epiphaneia*, meaning the visible manifestation of a deity. Paul is the only writer in the New Testament to use this word, which conveys a sense of the power of the presence of God. This leads into an equally powerful doxology to the immortal God "dwelling in unapproachable light" (v. 16).

Having written at length about the temptations and dangers of wealth, Paul closed with some advice to those who were already rich. He expressed himself again in terms of wealth versus contentment. The rich are not to "set their hope on the uncertainty of wealth, but on God, who richly provides us with all things to enjoy" (v. 17). The greatest value in wealth is sharing it so the rich "may take hold of life that is real" (v. 19).

In closing the letter, Paul reminded Timothy to "guard what has been entrusted to you" (v. 20). The blessings of being Jesus' disciple are too wonderful to be wasted. Certainly there are many Christians who fail to take advantage of their potential in God's kingdom. It seems as though Paul couldn't resist throwing in one more admonition, though there's no evidence at all that his hard-working young associate was ever tempted to do any less than his best.

For Your Consideration (6:13-21)

1. What was Paul's charge to Timothy?

2. What were Paul's instructions to people who are rich?

3. Who are some of the philanthropists who have made a difference in your community?

4. What do you think is the secret to becoming wealthy without becoming obsessed over money?

Chapter 7

The church's effectiveness

Scripture	2 Timothy 1:1–2:2

It's a good feeling when you know something you've done has made a difference. Whether it's a productive day at work, getting chores accomplished around the house, teaching a class, or coaching a team, it's great to know that what you did matters.

Think for a minute about your whole life, your whole career, or your entire witness for Christ. We all have a strong desire to look back at our lives or at specific experiences and say, "That counted for something." Paul took that kind of retrospective look at his life in his second letter to Timothy.

According to some scholars, Second Timothy is the last letter Paul wrote. He wrote it from a prison in Rome where he was awaiting news of his sentence from Nero, the emperor. (Paul died a martyr's death about A.D. 60.) It was a time of looking back and assessing a long life and ministry filled with travels and remarkable events. As Paul wrote, he considered and commented on the organization and ministry of the church in Ephesus.

Paul wanted the church to be effective, to make a difference, to mean something in the lives and hearts of the Ephesians. The elderly prisoner realized that his time was short and Timothy would be bearing the responsibility from that time forward. He wanted to keep the message energized and strong by suggesting what Timothy could do that would help him, other believers, and the church to minister effectively in the world. This priceless advice from an old and experienced evangelist is also intended for all of us.

For Your Consideration
1. Why is it we all want to believe we made a difference in the world?

2. What standards would you use to assess the impact of your life on others?

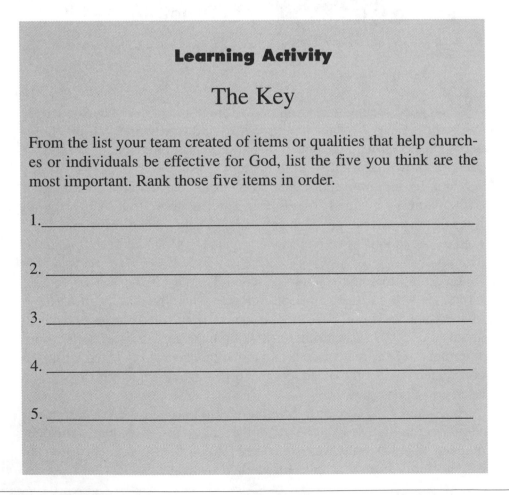

Learning Activity

The Key

From the list your team created of items or qualities that help churches or individuals be effective for God, list the five you think are the most important. Rank those five items in order.

1. _____

2. _____

3. _____

4. _____

5. _____

3. Who in the world today is making the biggest impact? How? What difference does that impact make to you?

Thanksgiving for Timothy's Faith
(2 Tim. 1:1-7)

I heard someone say once that he couldn't afford to buy cheap lumber. What he meant was that he couldn't afford to put time, energy, and money into a project around the house and then see it fall apart because it was made of cheap material. Cheap lumber may seem like a good idea at the time, but when it starts to warp or split, suddenly that expensive straight lumber seems like a much smarter buy.

Others say the same thing about clothes—well-made, long-lasting clothes are going to cost more than the ones that disintegrate in the washing machine after six months. In the long term, the more expensive choice is the most economical.

Paul reminded Timothy of his duty to serve the Lord completely, to the utmost of his ability. In God's economy Timothy couldn't afford to do a cheap job. Untrained, uncommitted, and unwilling believers set churches back more by wrong behavior than by doing nothing. Paul remembered Timothy's tears and his "sincere faith" (v. 5) as he recalled the times the two of them spent together in ministry. He reminded Timothy of his ability to serve on his own—not just as Paul's helper. He also reminded Timothy of the godly heritage found both in the teaching of his mother and grandmother (v. 5) and in the laying on of Paul's hands (v. 6). This ability to serve and the heritage of Christian teaching meant Timothy was equipped to succeed at his task.

It's interesting to note the difference in 1:6—where Paul mentioned "the laying on of my hands"—and a similar passage in 1 Timothy 4:14, "the laying on of hands by the council of elders." It may be that these

Mothers have the God-given opportunity to plant the first seeds of faith in a young life.

PhotoDisc

were two separate incidents, but it's more likely they were two descriptions of the same event. In the first one, the participation by all the elders is emphasized; in the second, Paul emphasized his personal relationship with Timothy.

If you're afraid to do something, you're not likely to do it very well. The most common reason for being afraid is fear of failure—you're about to try something you don't think you have the equipment or the knowledge to do successfully. This is especially true when it comes to sharing the gospel. As mentioned in an earlier lesson, very few Christians have the gift of sharing their faith comfortably. Witnessing to others is awkward, but it's awkward because few of us have been taught how to do it. With teaching comes confidence. Then with confidence the fear goes away.

For Your Consideration (1:1-7)
1. Who was responsible for bringing Timothy up in the Christian faith?

2. Why do you think Paul chose to describe a God-given spirit as "one of power, love, and sound judgment" (v. 7)?

3. How does being afraid affect your ability to accomplish something?

4. What is an example of a situation where you learned you couldn't afford to do a cheap job?

Boldly Proclaiming the Gospel (2 Tim. 1:8-10)

Along with Paul, Timothy had been waiting uneasily to learn what Nero's punishment for Paul would be. Timothy's faith was wavering under the stress of not knowing what would happen or when the decision would come. How would you feel if the teacher in whose footsteps you were following was in prison? It would certainly make me reconsider the value of his beliefs and the wisdom of dedicating my life to serving them.

Paul wrote: "So don't be ashamed of the testimony about our Lord, or of me His prisoner. Instead, share in suffering for the gospel, relying on the power of God" (v. 8). Paul was encouraging Timothy not to hold back out of timidity or indecision about the power of his message or out of embarrassment over Paul's imprisonment. There have been many times in my life when I needed a reminder like that. Situations come up that seem to hide God's presence and make it tough to take a stand for Christ. I've had those cynical questions and remarks tossed at me: *How many people go to church on Sunday anyway? If we all charge it to our expense accounts, no one will know the difference. All religions are alike. We all worship the same God.*

The natural tendency is to say nothing. How can you come back against such shallow and misguided thinking? But saying nothing speaks volumes about our faith and our commitment to serve Christ no matter what. The greater the pressure, the more important the stakes. But as Paul wrote in Galatians 3:27, "For as many of you as have been baptized into Christ have put on Christ." Christ is always with His people, even in moments of awkwardness, uncertainty, and fear. We need to pray faithfully to remember that our Savior will never leave us alone and defenseless if we will only call on Him.

Once Paul set up the subject of what it takes to witness effectively, he produced a detailed list of specific characteristics that make it possible. If you've ever wanted a checklist of what it takes to speak out successfully for Jesus, here it is:

Learning Activity

My Effectiveness

Effective ministry for God in the world is not judged by numbers, size of budgets, popularity, or any of the standards of measurement the world uses. Effectiveness in personal ministry for God, as God sees it, involves commitment, boldness, proclamation, faithfulness, and steadfastness. On the scales below, rate yourself in each of these areas. Pray for God to increase your personal ministry effectiveness for Him.

commitment	1	2	3	4	5	6	7	8	9	10
boldness	1	2	3	4	5	6	7	8	9	10
proclamation	1	2	3	4	5	6	7	8	9	10
faithfulness	1	2	3	4	5	6	7	8	9	10
steadfastness	1	2	3	4	5	6	7	8	9	10

Successful evangelists are bold and forthcoming in sharing their witness, not timid or embarrassed.

1. A "sincere faith" in the God of the Old Testament who has revealed Himself in Jesus (v. 5).
2. Keeping "ablaze the gift of God that is in you" so your passion for the Word never fails (v. 6).
3. A "spirit of fearlessness" that reflects the power of the Holy Spirit to conquer all evil (v. 7).
4. Power of the Holy Spirit to stand strong in the face of any test (v. 7).
5. Christian love that prevails over the evil in the world rather than answering hate with hate (v. 7).
6. The "sound judgment" of one who reasons and acts only out of obedience to God (v. 7).
7. Lack of any shame or indecision about our "testimony," but rather boldness in sharing our witness (v. 8).
8. Willingness to "share in suffering for the gospel," knowing that God honors every sacrifice made in His name (v. 8).
9. "Relying on the power of God," because no other power is enough to prevail over every obstacle (v. 8).

For Your Consideration (1:8-10)

1. How was Timothy supposed to feel about Paul's being a prisoner?

2. Why was Paul called to suffer?

3. How would you feel following the leadership of someone who was arrested and put in prison?

4. What are some cynical questions or comments you've heard about Christianity? What did you do in response?

5. Based on Paul's list, how effective are you in speaking out for Christ? What steps can you take to improve?

6. Who is the most effective Christian witness you know personally? What makes that person successful?

Remaining True to the Faith (2 Tim. 1:11-18)

Here Paul wrote of his appointment as "a herald, apostle, and teacher" of the gospel (v. 11). This is the same gospel that got him thrown in prison and otherwise made his life so difficult. Yet he was unashamed of his condition as a prisoner. To Paul, faith was an unwavering lifetime commitment to Christ, who would guard what had "been entrusted to" him—his testimony and all those he had influenced for salvation—until the day of Christ's return to earth.

You can almost feel Paul's wish to be with his young friend as he encouraged him to "hold on" to the teaching he had received (v. 13) and guard "that good thing entrusted" to him (v. 14). Paul could not be there in person to encourage and exhort, so he had to rely on words written in a prison cell to carry his thoughts and convey the depth of his emotions. "That good thing" Timothy had been entrusted with was what both of them had dedicated their lives to—the truth of the gospel.

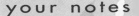

While many in Asia had deserted Paul since he became a prisoner (here "Asia" means the Roman province of Asia Minor), he reported that Onesiphorus and his household had never failed him. From the description in verse 16 it's clear that Onesiphorus visited Paul in jail. In fact this man, who was an Ephesian, risked his life traveling to Rome to see Paul and to help him minister to the other prisoners. When Paul wrote from his cell, Onesiphorus was probably on his way back to Ephesus from Rome. Paul wrote about his visit in the past tense, which indicates it was over, but sent greetings to his household and not to him. Either Paul didn't feel the need to greet Onesiphorus himself since they had visited so recently, or Onesiphorus hadn't made it home yet. For his selfless service, Onesiphorus was sure to "obtain mercy from the Lord on that day" when he stood before the throne of the Lord to render an account of himself (v. 18).

Chapter 2 then begins with a call for Timothy to stand "strong in the grace that is Christ Jesus" (v. 1) and to see his position as one who passed the knowledge of Christianity on to other people, who then in turn taught it to other people. Like concentric rings in a pool, the message of the gospel was thus spread wider and wider. That is evangelism in a nutshell.

For Your Consideration (1:11-18)

1. What did Paul encourage Timothy to "hold on to"?

2. What was Timothy instructed to guard?

3. Why does it seem harder to convince somebody to do something in writing than it does in person?

The church's suffering

Scripture	2 Timothy 2:3-26

Teachers spend a lot of time repeating themselves because repetition is one of a teacher's best tools. Kids in school hear dates and facts and multiplication tables repeated over and over again until they're second nature. Musicians and athletes practice the same movement countless times to nail down specialized skills. In writing to Timothy, Paul came back to a few key points time and again. His topics are familiar to us too by now. He told his youthful associate not to be self-conscious about being young. He reminded him that sound doctrine is important, as was Timothy's personal reputation as a pastor and leader. Paul encouraged him to be strong, confident, and clear in his faith.

This lesson introduces a new and thought-provoking topic—Christians are called to suffer for their faith. Paul wrote that we should all share the sufferings of Christ as though he assumed there would be suffering to share. It isn't a question of *if,* but *when.*

The "suffering of Christ" is a hard concept to talk about. Who wants to be part of a religion that warns you to expect to suffer for your faith? Nobody likes to suffer, because suffering implies weakness, failure, and inadequacy. But suffering is a major theme in Christian history, and it remains part of the Christian experience today. By some estimates there are more than 250,000 Christians around the world murdered for their faith every year in the 21st century, far more than died during the bloodiest days of the Roman Empire.

Yet no one suffered more than Jesus, who died a torturous death on a cross to atone for the sins of the world. A perfect God chose to take human form and to experience the worst kind of human suffering. That is the example for Christians to follow. There are two kingdoms on earth: God's and Satan's. Until the Lord returns, there will be suffering among His people. The stronger and surer Christians are, the more Satan will work to make their lives miserable and to drive them from God.

For Your Consideration

1. How is Christian suffering today similar to what it was in Timothy's time? How is it different?

2. How do you explain suffering when you talk about your faith?

3. Why do you think Paul waited until so late in his letter to mention Christian suffering?

Strength in the Face of Suffering (2 Tim. 2:3-13)

In taking on a bigger share of the ministry in Ephesus, Timothy was bound to take on a bigger share of the difficulty. Paul used the imagery of a soldier, an athlete, and a farmer—all hard workers at difficult tasks—as examples of those who share in suffering with resolve and determination.

A soldier (v. 3) places himself under the command of others and fights to the death if ordered to do so. A soldier also lives and works apart from the citizens he serves and follows a different, more stringent set of rules. Christians live in the world, but are not of the world. Christian leaders have a calling and responsibility that require them to look above "the concerns of everyday life" (v. 4) to a higher level of purpose and accountability.

Just as an athlete must compete "according to the rules" (v. 5), Timothy had to experience the rigors of a disciplined life to have a successful ministry. There are no shortcuts to rigorous physical training and following the rules of the game in order to win. In the same way, there are no shortcuts to spiritual maturity and effectiveness.

The farmer has a right to be "the first to get a share of the crops" (v. 6). The metaphor of the harvest is used often in the Bible to represent the mission field. Farmers work hard to enjoy the fruit of their labors. Evangelists and church leaders labor for a harvest of souls. Effective servants of Christ carry out their duties with focus, discipline, and persistent hard work. Timothy was on his own now, and whatever standards he achieved in these areas would come from his own sense of self-motivation.

"Consider what I say," Paul wrote in verse 7, "for the Lord will give you understanding in everything." A quick reading of this passage might make you think he was saying that the Lord will enable you to understand everything there is to know. Reading closer,

Paul compared the work of Christians to that of a soldier, an athlete, and a farmer.

978

Images by Getty

Learning Activity

Me, Suffer?

Second Timothy 2:3 calls us to "share in the suffering" of Christ. Describe your feelings about suffering or being persecuted for your faith. How have you experienced persecution or suffering as a Christian?

the meaning becomes clear: "the Lord will give you understanding" in everything I've said and which I'm asking you to "consider."

Writing from prison in Rome, Paul was very much aware of his confinement, to the point of being shackled as he wrote. He suffered by "being bound like a criminal" (v. 9), yet found comfort in knowing that the message of God was not bound. Jesus rose from the dead as the Old Testament prophets promised according to what Paul called "my gospel" (v. 8). Every prophecy came true, and that truth is worth suffering for. His suffering also benefits others chosen by God "so that they also may obtain salvation" (v. 10).

Christians and people looking into Christianity hear a lot about the blessings of the gospel and the peace and assurance that comes with salvation in Jesus. But the church, especially in North America, has been hesitant to lift up what Paul wrote to the Philippians: "For it has been given you on Christ's behalf not only to believe in Him, but also to suffer for Him" (Phil. 1:29). Being a Christian isn't easy and won't necessarily make you comfortable. Christ suffered, and suffering is part of the calling of all believers. Even the act of enduring hardship in the name of Jesus can demonstrate the power of Christian faith. Suffering in Christ is never in vain.

Paul followed this series of thoughts with a hymn telling his readers that even the darkest trials have their rewards. If we die in serving Christ "we will also live with Him" (v. 11) and "will also reign with Him" (v. 12). He added the warning that "if we deny Him, He will also deny us" (v. 12), but if we fail and lose our faith, Jesus "remains faithful, for He cannot deny Himself" (v. 13). The Lord is faithful to us even when we're weak and deny Him.

IN DEPTH

Leadership and Responsibility

In biblical times, as well as today, the greater leadership role a person has, the more responsibility he or she must shoulder. As a soldier moves up in the ranks to command more troops, he is responsible for more lives. A political leader is granted power with the expectation that she will accept responsibility for the safety and welfare of the people she represents. Imagine Moses and his responsibility for thousands of his people wandering in the desert who depended on him for everything. Leaders need our unending prayers for wisdom, courage, and discernment.

For Your Consideration (2:3-13)

1. What does it mean to be "in the world but not of the world"?

2. To what kinds of people did Paul compare Christians? Why did he pick those particular ones?

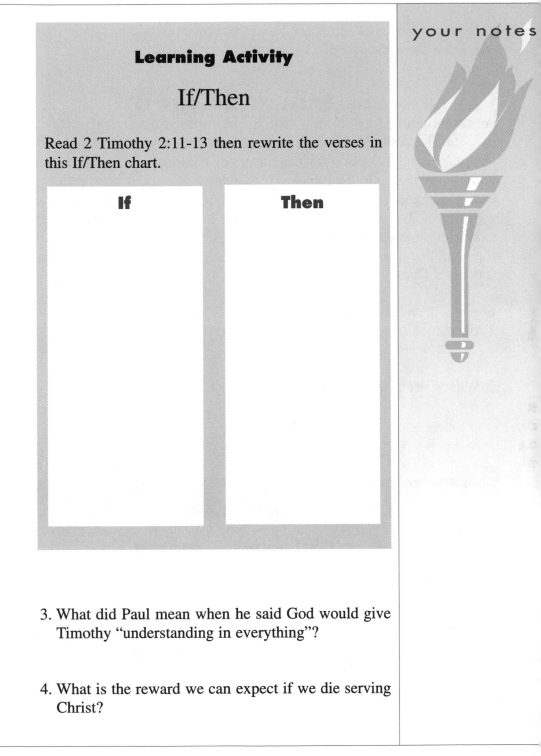

Learning Activity

If/Then

Read 2 Timothy 2:11-13 then rewrite the verses in this If/Then chart.

If	Then

3. What did Paul mean when he said God would give Timothy "understanding in everything"?

4. What is the reward we can expect if we die serving Christ?

5. What are some of the possible consequences of talking with your friends about the idea of Christian suffering?

A Good Worker (2 Tim. 2:14-15)

After this uplifting hymn, Paul shifted gears to a more practical series of thoughts that further refined his image of what effective Christian workers must be. They can't get caught up in pointless arguments about words. And they must be diligent. If they have done their best, whatever the outcome, if they have taught correctly, they have nothing to be ashamed of. The word "correctly" (v. 15) is interesting because it comes from the same Greek word as "orthodontist" and originally described road building in a straight line. Paul saw Timothy teaching in a straightforward manner without distractions and disputes.

For Your Consideration (2:14-15)
1. How did Paul say Christians should behave?

2. What's wrong with Christians disagreeing over words?

IN DEPTH

When Christians Disagree

Paul admonished Christians not to waste their time in argument, yet it is important to explore the meaning of Scripture and how best to follow the teachings of Jesus. Healthy debate is beneficial in that it helps uncover the truth. But selfish argument is a waste because the goal isn't finding the truth—it's wearing the other person down and getting your way. This is the kind of pointless argument Paul was warning against.

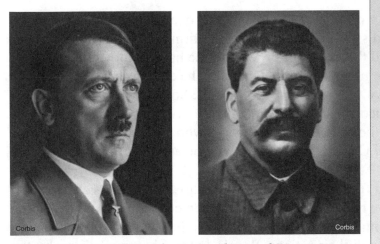

Corbis   Corbis

Powerful persuaders who twist the truth are among the most evil figures in history.

3. What's the best way to head off an argument between Christians over terminology?

Dangers of Twisting the Truth
(2 Tim 2:16-26)

A persuasive speaker spewing forth falsehood is one of the world's most dangerous forces. The great villains of the 20th century—Hitler and Stalin—come to mind, and a long list of ruthless dictators who followed them. This is what happens when powerful persuaders lead their followers off in the wrong direction.

But powerful preachers proclaiming the true Word of God are special instruments of His service in the world. Those who twist the truth are ultimately destroyed. Those who hold fast to the gospel may suffer earthly trials, but their ultimate reward will be great.

Paul gave examples of his own of people who had spoken falsehoods, whose lies "will spread like gangrene" (v. 17), so that instead of reaching ever outward from one circle of believers to the next with the truth of God, Hymenaeus and Philetus infected their listeners with the deadly disease of falsehood. But once again, even in spite of their lies, "God's solid foundation [stood] firm" (v. 19).

As Paul used the metaphor of reaping the harvest for Christian evangelism, here he turned to the metaphor of the church as a "large house" (v. 20) filled with two categories of dishes. Some were gold and silver, reserved for special use, while others were everyday wood and clay. In the same way, the church contains people who are specially used to contain the truth of Christ along with others who are unworthy because they are untruthful.

Returning to further characteristics of Christian workers and leaders, Paul focused on how to behave. Faith and practice are intertwined to the point where faith guides the behavior of the faithful, and others can see their faith through their actions. People judge what you believe by the way you act even more than by what you say. Avoiding "youthful passions" and turning instead to "righteousness, faith, love, and peace" is a sermon by example—one of the best sermons of all.

The best teachers do more than repeat the facts over and over: they direct others to discover the truth on their own. A teacher's goal isn't to win an argument but to lead. The final result of a Christian teacher's work will be for his hearers to "come to their senses and escape the Devil's trap" (v. 26)—the trap of a ruined life laid waste by useless discussions and quarrels.

For Your Consideration (2:16-26)

1. What sort of speech should Christians avoid? Why?

2. What kind of examples were Hymenaeus and Philetus?

3. What did Paul warn Timothy to flee from?

4. How must the Lord's slaves behave?

5. What are some consequences of twisting the truth in today's world?

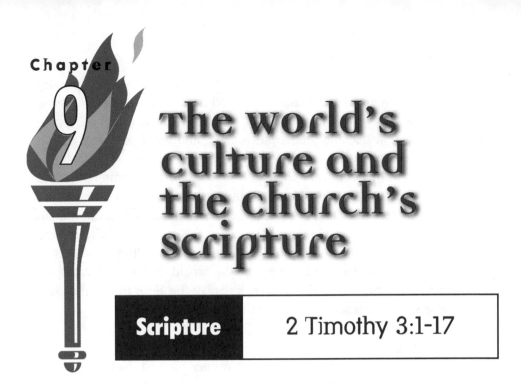

The world's culture and the church's scripture

Scripture	2 Timothy 3:1-17

O ne of the issues that defines our culture is the argument whether there are absolute standards of truth and morality. On one side of the question, everybody is supposed to accept one universal standard. On the other, each person sets a standard based on his individual beliefs, preferences, and experience.

Imagine for a minute how absolutely impossible it would be to drive if everybody decided individually what the standards would be. One person thinks 50 miles an hour is fast enough, but the car behind is convinced the minimum speed should be at least 80. One group drives on the right-hand side of the street while others prefer the left. The result would be carnage and chaos, and nobody would get anywhere.

The same is true when it comes to the cultural and moral climate of the nation. Until relatively recently, American society recognized a universal standard of moral behavior founded on courtesy, order, and propriety. It was expected in school, on public streets, at entertainment events, and everywhere else people gathered together.

But in the mid-1960s public morality underwent a drastic transformation. Previous standards were suddenly declared irrelevant and judgmental. "You can't tell me how to act!" became the new cry in favor of individual rights. Before this time the church and the community at large held to the same standard of behavior. Even those who weren't regular churchgoers recognized the value in shared standards. After all, those standards were as old as the first settlements in America, and they produced a nation that became the freest, richest, and most powerful nation in the history of the world.

Throughout all this cultural upheaval, the true church remains a rock of consistency. There are many temptations—especially in the effort to attract new seekers to Christ—to change the culture of the church, to make it more attractive and more relevant. But the message of Christ, and the message of Paul to Timothy in 2 Timothy 3, is that the church is to stand apart from the decadent culture of the world. No matter what the moral climate of the world, the church lives by the Scriptures, and they alone are the Christian standard for faith and practice.

For Your Consideration

1. How can you respond to someone who argues against the existence of absolute standards of truth and morality?

2. How can churches change and modernize to meet the needs of contemporary society without losing sight of Christian absolutes?

3. How did Paul use what had happened in the past to plan for the future? How can your church do that?

Cultural Christianity (2 Tim. 3:1-5)

The description of people Paul warned Timothy to avoid in the opening verses of chapter 3 has changed little if at all since the first century A.D. This list of 19 personality traits could as easily describe almost any criminal on the evening news. Another disturbing type of person then and now is the cultural Christian, someone who goes to church as a social activity but puts nothing into it and gets nothing out of it. In a way, these are the most dangerous types of all, because on the outside they do what Christians do—go to church, read the Bible, sing hymns and praise songs—but on the inside they're living strictly for themselves. In short, while professing to be Christians, they express the opposite in their lives, attitudes, and actions.

The one word in Paul's list of 19 characteristics that may best describe the cultural Christian is "traitor" (v. 4). A traitor puts his or her own interests before country or anything else and destroys secretly from within. The people described here are lovers of the wrong things, and "lovers of pleasure rather than lovers of God" (v. 4).

It's worth stopping for a minute to think about our own behavior and attitudes toward the church. Do you look for the lost as Jesus did, or do you let them go? Do you work to bring Christian unity to your church

your notes

Learning Activity

What About Me?

On the list below, circle the words or phrases that others might use to describe you. Underline the words or phrases that represent things you want to eliminate from your life.

lover of self

lover of money

boastful

proud

blasphemer

disobedient to parents

ungrateful

unholy

unloving

irreconcilable

slanderers

without self-control

brutal

without love for what
　is good

traitor

reckless

conceited

lover of pleasure

fellowship or leave that up to somebody else? It's possible to get in the way of church evangelism and teaching without meaning to. Be on guard to insure you avoid the symptoms of cultural Christianity.

Think also about what your church does and why. Many Christian churches today have drifted away from biblical standards of behavior and worship to become popular in the community or to increase their attendance. They've decided to let the secular culture dictate what the church should do. That attitude is dangerously at odds with the teachings of Christ.

Learning Activity

Profitable Scripture

"All Scripture is inspired by God and is profitable for teaching, for rebuking, for correcting, for training in righteousness, so that the man of God may be complete, equipped for every good work" (2 Tim. 3:16-17).

List one way Scripture can be used for each action:

• teaching

• rebuking

• correcting

• training in righteousness

• equipped for every good work

False teachers claim power for themselves, not power in the name of Jesus.

For Your Consideration (3:1-5)

1. What kind of world should Christians expect in the future? What kinds of people will live in it?

2. Do you agree that "traitor" is the best of Paul's terms for describing a cultural Christian? If so, explain why. If not, what term is better?

3. Why is a cultural Christian more hazardous to the faith than a nonbeliever?

False Leaders and False Promises (2 Tim. 3:6-10)

About all we know of Jannes and Jambres, the two men mentioned in verse 8, is that they were magicians in the service of the Egyptian pharaoh and they opposed the godly teachings of Moses. What could be worse than to go down in history as a biblical example of how not to behave?

These two men represent the many people who cling to false religion. Surrounded by the trappings of magic and the occult, Jannes and Jambres are among those who "resist the truth" (v. 8) because the truth will rob them of personal power and force them to acknowledge that all power comes from God.

This quest for power is also what prompts followers of false religions to take advantage of the spiritually or

PhotoDisc

morally weak—"idle women" who are "led along by a variety of passions" (v. 6). They can't claim the true power of God, so they act and command in their own power, which leads their followers to ruin.

Our world is full of false religious leaders who claim the power to make their followers rich, to cure their illnesses, or to somehow make life easy for them. Even churches today often worry more about acceptance and membership growth than they do preaching the biblical truth.

Paul himself is an example of the fact that Christians are never promised an easy life on earth. On the contrary, they're taught to expect just the opposite. In the short run it's not difficult to attract followers by promising them things that satisfy their fallen and selfish human nature. But those false prophets eventually lead only to disappointment and despair while the true Christ lights the path to eternal life.

For Your Consideration (3:6-10)
1. Who were Jannes and Jambres?

2. Why are people in today's culture so eager to follow false spiritual teaching?

3. What can Christians do to neutralize the influence of false teaching?

Paul's Example (2 Tim. 3:11-13)

The stronger your faith is, the more it will be tested. Paul was one of the greatest Christian leaders of all time, and he suffered mightily. "What persecutions I endured!" he wrote with passion in verse 11. Persecution may be the best evidence of all that you are living a Christlike like. "In fact," Paul affirmed, " all those who want to live a godly life in Christ Jesus will be persecuted" (v. 12).

Paul's persecutions are described in Acts 13 and 14, beginning when the Holy Spirit set him and Barnabas apart to do His special work. Paul traveled to Antioch, Iconium, and Lystra preaching the gospel. But the more successful he was, the more he was persecuted: expelled from Antioch by the Jews (Acts 13:50), threatened with assault in Iconium

(Acts 14:5), and stoned and left for dead in Lystra (Acts 14:19).

Paul was a man who lived faithfully and frugally, acting in a way that illustrated his beliefs. He didn't live comfortably while asking others to sacrifice. He didn't claim power in the name of Jesus, then try to imply that anything he did was out of his own strength and wisdom. Paul's sacrifice gave him the authority to tell others how to live their lives. By giving his all to Jesus, he could claim Jesus' infinite power to speak through him.

For Your Consideration (3:11-13)

1. Where was Paul persecuted during his ministry?

2. What kind of dangers did Paul face on his journeys?

IN DEPTH

Punishment

Stoning is mentioned often in the Bible and was a common and brutal way of punishing or executing someone accused of a crime such as adultery or heresy. The accused was surrounded by townspeople who threw stones at him until he was knocked unconscious or killed. Stoning is still practiced in some Muslim countries today. Crucifixion was an even more grisly death because it took hours to die. Condemned people nailed to a cross slowly suffocated as they became too weak to pull themselves up by the nails in their wrists in order to breathe. It was against the law to crucify Roman citizens because such a death was considered too humiliating.

your notes

3. What will happen to those who live a godly life?

4. Why do you think Paul dwelt on his persecutions and suffering?

5. What does Paul's example teach us about our own lives as witnesses for Christ?

God's Inspired Word (2 Tim. 3:14-17)

In two sentences, beginning with verse 14, Paul pointed out with incredible brevity and clarity the purposes of Scripture as he had learned it over many years of service to Christ and had it revealed to him by the Lord. Scripture is "able to instruct you for salvation through faith in Christ Jesus" (v. 15). This is a foundational truth that separates Christianity from every

Stoning is a brutal form of punishment or execution still practiced in the Middle East and other areas.

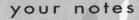

other religion and the inerrant Bible from all other sources of religious instruction. Christians should be familiar with the Bible and build on that unshakable foundation for a lifetime.

All of the Bible is "inspired by God" (v. 16) and is "profitable for teaching, for rebuking, for correcting, for training in righteousness, so that the man of God may be complete, equipped for every good word" (vv. 16). The Greek word for "inspire" literally means "God-breathed" or "breathed out by God." There's no stronger or more powerful image of the origin of the Bible than its being the breath of the God who created everything that is. This idea is reinforced by 2 Peter 1:20-21: "First of all, you should know this: no prophecy of Scripture comes from one's own interpretation, because no prophecy ever came by the will of man; instead, moved by the Holy Spirit, men spoke from God."

This inspired, God-breathed teaching is ours so we may "be complete, equipped for every good work" (v. 17). "Man of God" is used in this verse in a generic sense. All the same "people" in verse 2 who were lovers of so many evil attributes can be transformed, completed, and equipped by God's Word.

For Your Consideration (3:14-17)

1. What are the most important purposes of Scripture?

2. What is the origin of all Scripture?

3. What risk do you run in measuring everything you hear against the Word of God?

4. Why did Paul put such emphasis on Scripture at this point in his message?

Chapter 10

The Lord's Return and the church's proclamation

Scripture	2 Timothy 4:1-22

T he last chapter of Second Timothy has a feel of finality to it, as though the apostle Paul knew somehow that this would be the last part of the last letter he would ever write. Both the intensity and the subject matter have a sense of importance and urgency.

Of course there's no way to know for sure whether Paul thought this would be the last of his legacy of epistles, but the circumstances surrounding it are rich with emotion. He was an old man who had traveled and suffered a great deal in the service of Christ. He was in prison and likely to die there. He was writing to a young energetic associate who was preparing to carry on with the work of evangelism after Paul's death. His solemn words were a heartfelt combination of instruction and encouragement.

If you had a feeling that a certain message would be the last one you would ever send, what would you put into it? What would you talk about, and how would you express it? We hear accounts of terminally ill patients or condemned prisoners—people who know their time remaining is short—that range from expressions of anger, defiance, and hatred, to instruction, to almost transcendent love and peacefulness.

The way someone expresses himself near the end of his life depends on several things. First is his attitude about the world and his place in it. Second is how important it is to him that his message be passed along to those who follow. And third, when his life is over, what does he believe comes afterward? In all these areas Paul is one of the Bible's great examples of the Christian outlook.

For Your Consideration

1. If you could sum up Paul's message to Timothy in a few words, what would they be?

2. If you knew a letter you were writing would be your last one ever, what would you say?

3. What are some "famous last words" that impressed or inspired you?

Proclaiming Christ (2 Tim. 4:1-6)

Paul wrote with a powerful sense of purpose. "I solemnly charge you: proclaim the message; persist in it whether convenient or not; rebuke, correct, and encourage with great patience and teaching" (vv. 1-2). Here Paul's message in his two letters to Timothy came full circle. He began the first letter by focusing on the church's transforming gospel. Now he concluded the second by emphasizing the process of making disciples through Christian proclamation.

In this closing summary Paul turned again to the idea that proclaiming the gospel isn't easy, but that Christians are called to persist in their effort "whether convenient or not" (v. 2). Rebuking and correcting as Paul instructed isn't likely to win any popularity

your notes

Proclaiming the gospel isn't easy, but Paul called on Timothy to persist in his effort "whether convenient or not" (v. 2).

contests. We all naturally want to avoid offending or irritating people. But in our time, taking or defending a strongly Christian point of view on any issue has become politically incorrect. Popular culture seems eager to erase even the most watered-down references to Christianity in public debate, matters of morality, guidance for government leaders, and even in Christmas, where the Christmas season has become "the holidays" and includes every sort of pointless secular festivity and non-Christian celebration.

Across the centuries Paul is calling us to proclaim the Christian message in our world, to stand up for the absolute truth of the Bible against all comers. Unless we do, our culture will reveal "an itch to hear something new" (v. 3) the same way Timothy's did. As an alternate reading of that phrase, the *Holman Christian Standard Bible*® has "an itch to hear what they want to hear." In other words, unless they hear the truth, they'll go off in another direction that suits their selfish interests.

For Your Consideration (4:1-6)

1. What was Paul's "solemn charge" to Timothy?

2. What advice did Timothy receive in this passage?

3. How do you think the difference in their ages affected Paul's instructions and Timothy's understanding of them?

4. What are some ways you can hold on to the courage to stand up for the gospel even when it's difficult?

IN DEPTH

The Heavenly Kingdom

In 4:1, Paul charged Timothy in the name of God's appearing and "His kingdom." In verse 18 he shared the assurance that the Lord would bring him "safely into His heavenly kingdom." These are the only two places in the pastoral epistles where the kingdom of God is mentioned. Verse 1 combines the images of "His appearing and His kingdom" in a form called *hendiadys*, which is two words connected by a conjunction in a way that represents a complex idea. The second mention, in verse 18, is a straightforward and soothing expression of the "heavenly kingdom" that awaits all of Christ's faithful servants.

Rewards for the Faithful (2 Tim. 4:6-8)

Paul's reference to a sacrificial "drink offering" (v. 6) recalls a similar passage in his letter to the Philippians when he wrote, "But even if I am poured out as a drink offering on the sacrifice and service of your faith, I am glad and rejoice with all of you" (Phil. 2:17). This is an Old Testament concept, referring to God's instruction to Moses that the children of Israel must make a drink offering to Him when they arrived into the land He promised them (Num. 15:1-12; 28:7,24). This was an expression by Paul that he believed his journey in the service of God was nearing an end.

Paul had "finished the race" (v. 7) and could say that he had "fought the good fight" and "kept the faith" through all the trials set before him. This was both a challenge and encouragement to Timothy who had much work and many tests of faith still ahead of him.

How can you as a Christian fight the good fight and keep the faith as you run your race in the secular culture? Will you earn the "crown of righteousness" (v. 8) that Paul was sure he would receive? You can, Paul assured us, because the same reward and recognition will be awarded "to all those who have loved His appearing" (v. 8).

Learning Activity

Last Words

If you had one last opportunity to share some personal thoughts before the end of your life, what would be the last thing you would want to say?

What types of things do people include in their last words to others?

"I have finished the race" (2 Tim. 4:7).
Paul knew he had little time left.

Getty Images

For Your Consideration (4:6-8)

1. What did Paul claim as his accomplishments in serving Christ?

2. What would be Paul's reward for his faithfulness?

3. What do you expect your reward to be for your Christian service?

4. How can you "run the race" for your faith even in today's secular culture?

Followers in the Faith (2 Tim. 4:9-18)

Paul's loneliness breaks through here in the form of a request for Timothy to visit him at the prison in Rome. He mentioned four other followers who had left him.

Though three of them—Crescens, Titus, and Tychicus—had gone to ministry assignments elsewhere, Demas had deserted him "because he loved this present world" (v. 10). The three faithful associates had gone on to multiply Paul's ministry, but one fell by the wayside.

He also mentioned other colleagues: Luke, who was with him in Rome (v. 11); Mark, whom Paul asked Timothy to bring with him when he came to visit (v. 11); and Carpus, who had stored some of Paul's belongings for safekeeping, including some valuable parchments (v. 13). Alexander the coppersmith was singled out as one who "did great harm" but who would be repaid by the Lord "according to his works" (v. 14).

The Mark who is mentioned in verse 11 was John Mark, who turned back on Paul's first missionary journey (see Acts 13 and 15), and whom Paul refused to take on his second trip. The fact that this man was "useful" is an encouragement to anyone who has ever failed in the service of Christ. There is forgiveness, and there will be other opportunities.

Paul's list of acquaintances reminds us that there are many times when Christians have to choose between enjoying the company of others and remaining true to Christian standards. Paul's loneliness as a prisoner was an extreme case. But he endured it willingly, as he had so many other hardships, in the service of his Savior.

For Your Consideration (4:9-18)

1. Who was staying with Paul as he wrote?

2. What two people did Paul mention who had failed either as ministers or as companions?

3. Who alone stood with Paul at his "first defense"?

4. Do you think Paul's mention of "the lion's mouth" is literal or metaphorical?

5. What evidence do you have that you will one day enter the Lord's "heavenly kingdom"?

Learning Activity

The Race

On the scale below, indicate how well you are presently running the race of faith. Are you running a good race and fighting a good fight of faith?

| 1 | | 10 |

What are some of the hurdles keeping you from running the best race possible?

What are examples of things that have tripped you up in your race of faith?

On this scale, indicate how well you would like to be running the race of faith this time next year.

| 1 | | 10 |

What are some specific things you can do to help you reach this goal?

What hurdles do you anticipate you will have to navigate to reach your goal?

Paul's Parting Benediction
(2 Tim. 4:19-22)

Paul's letters to Timothy reveal a man who kept the faith in the face of overwhelming odds. In his own weakness he was powerless, but with Christ he had the power to accomplish great things for the faith.

"Grace be with you" (v. 22) was Paul's personal farewell. At the same time Paul's ministry was nearing its end, there were clearly many people, including young Timothy, ready to pick up where the apostle left off. As the great preacher and reformer John Wesley said, "God buries His workmen, but His work goes on."

Kingdom-anticipating churches and believers are committed to fulfilling their ministries until they go to be with the Lord or until the Lord returns for them. Only when we devote ourselves to the Great Commission can we fulfill our Christian calling until the Lord returns. By holding Paul up as a wise and devoted teacher and seeing Timothy as an energetic, self-sacrificing, obedient student, we get a clear picture of what churches and evangelism are all about.

We are called to share the gospel as long as we can as often as we can and to equip others to reach out to the next level and the next generation with the saving message of Jesus Christ.

For Your Consideration (4:19-22)

1. How did Paul close his letters?

2. What about the relationship between Paul and Timothy characterizes the passing of God's message from one generation to the next?

3. How have Paul's letters to Timothy changed your outlook on Christian witness? What will you do differently from now on?

CHRISTIAN GROWTH STUDY PLAN

Preparing Christians to Serve

In the Christian Growth Study Plan (formerly Church Study Course), this book **The Church Anticipating the Kingdom: Studies in 1 & 2 Timothy** is a resource for course credit in one Leadership and Skill Development diploma and two Christian Growth diploma plans. To receive credit, read the book, complete the learning activities, show your work to your pastor, a staff member or church leader, then complete the information on the next page. The form may be duplicated. Send the completed page to:

Christian Growth Study Plan
One LifeWay Plaza
Nashville, TN 37234-0117
FAX: (615)251-5067
Email: cgspnet@lifeway.com

For information about the Christian Growth Study Plan, refer to the current Christian Growth Study Plan Catalog. Your church office may have a copy. If not, request a free copy from the Christian Growth Study Plan office (615/251-2525). Also available online at www.lifeway.com/cgsp/catalog.

The Church Anticipating the Kingdom: Studies in 1 & 2 Timothy

☐ CG-0802   ☐ LS-0053 (Sunday School)

PARTICIPANT INFORMATION

Social Security Number (USA ONLY-optional)

Personal CGSP Number*

Date of Birth (MONTH, DAY, YEAR)

Name (First, Middle, Last)

Home Phone

Address (Street, Route, or P.O. Box)

City, State, or Province

Zip/Postal Code

CHURCH INFORMATION

Church Name

Address (Street, Route, or P.O. Box)

City, State, or Province

Zip/Postal Code

CHANGE REQUEST ONLY

☐ Former Name

☐ Former Address

City, State, or Province

Zip/Postal Code

☐ Former Church

City, State, or Province

Zip/Postal Code

Signature of Pastor, Conference Leader, or Other Church Leader

Date

*New participants are requested but not required to give SS# and date of birth. Existing participants, please give CGSP# when using SS# for the first time. Thereafter, only one ID# is required. **Mail to:** Christian Growth Study Plan, One LifeWay Plaza, Nashville, TN 37234-0117. Fax: (615)251-5067.

Rev.   5-02